Rays of Hope

Finding Hope in Seemingly Hopeless Situations

ROSIE RIVERA

WestBow
PRESS
A DIVISION OF THOMAS NELSON

Scripture taken from the New King James Version. Copyright 1979, 1980, 1982 by Thomas Nelson, inc. Used by permission. All rights reserved.

One Scripture quote taken from the Amplified Bible, Copyright © 1954, 1958, 1962, 1964, 1965, 1987 by The Lockman Foundation. Used by permission.

WestBow Press books may be ordered through booksellers or by contacting:

WestBow Press
A Division of Thomas Nelson
1663 Liberty Drive
Bloomington, IN 47403
www.westbowpress.com
1-(866) 928-1240

ISBN: 978-1-4497-2318-7 (sc)
ISBN: 978-1-4497-2319-4 (e)

Library of Congress Control Number: 2011914735

Printed in the United States of America

WestBow Press rev. date: 09/15/2011

Forward

It is an honor for me to write the forward for Rays of Hope. Rosie Rivera is one of my dearest friends whom God divinely placed in my life sixteen years ago. She is a warm and compassionate woman of God. She radiates God's love, peace and gentleness. She has always been there to give a listening ear when I need encouragement or godly counsel concerning the church my husband and I pastor. She has had more experience pastoring so I have confidence that she will give good advice when needed.

Rosie is an anointed teacher of the word. She has ministered with love and compassion to our women at First His Kingdom church for over fifteen years. The women of our church look forward to hearing her teach the word with confirmation following.

I highly recommend Rays of Hope. As you read it you will sense God's love and peace. I believe that all of us face hopeless situations in our life at one time or another. You will find comfort as you read this book. You will sense the tangible presence of God comforting you and wrapping his loving arms around you with a blanket of his precious love. You will be transformed in your mind, your heart and your emotions. As you read you will sense the presence of God. Rays of Hope is filled with the word and the anointing.

I believe this is an awakening of Rosie Rivera's writing gift which has been in her since the foundation of the world for such a time as this.

I also recommend Rosie's first book Stolen Identity. With so much chaos going on in the world it's good to know that God is speaking to our hearts through books like this. Too many children of God have trouble knowing who they are in Christ and why they were created. We will begin the most wonderful journey of our life when we allow Jesus to be our Lord and Savior. Only then will we truly find our true identity in Christ Jesus and can leave our past behind and look forward to fulfilling God's plan and destiny for our life. Stolen Identity is a book based on scripture. It is uncomplicated and easy to read. Through it we understand the many struggles we have faced in the past.

Rays of Hope in like manner will encourage you to have confidence in the fact that you are more than a conqueror and you can make it in this world knowing that God loves you and his love is ever enduring. You are the righteousness of God in Christ.

Pastor Rose Zepeda
First His Kingdom Church
Pflugerville, Texas

Acknowledgements

I give all the praise and glory to my Lord and Savior Jesus Christ who has graced me with the ability to write poetry. It is he who places the poems in my heart. I know without a doubt that without God's grace I am limited in what I can do. I depend wholly upon his grace.

My husband Robert also had a big role to play in the writing of this book. He is the one who encouraged me to put these poems in book form. He is my number one fan and my greatest supporter. I praise God for such a wonderful man.

I also want to acknowledge my good friend Rose who wrote the forward to this book. She is a beautiful person and a great friend. God brought her into my life several years ago. Many people come and go throughout our lives but there are some that I believe are divine appointments which God arranges, Rose is one of them. I thank God for friends like her.

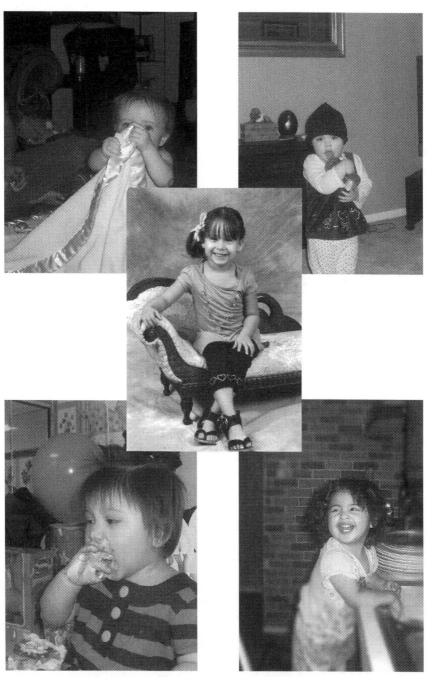

I dedicate this book to my grandchildren Addison,
Analiyah, Jolynn, Reyna, and Antigone.

Introduction

Poetry is a language of the heart. It has a way of expressing one's innermost feelings. It's one of the greatest means of expression one has.

People write for different reasons, for some it's a way of expressing their innermost thoughts and feelings, for others it's a way of releasing emotion, for others it's a gift one is born with, poetry comes natural to that person.

Poetry is a very powerful tool. People use it as a means of expressing thoughts and ideas. At times the thoughts from ones heart are designed to encourage others, other times it's a means of making people think and other times the poet simply wants to share something that touched his or her heart in some special way. At times people will express a deep seated hurt of things they are experiencing in their own life through poetry.

Most of the poems in this book are meant to encourage the reader, some are written from personal experiences. They are a means of giving people hope when situations seem hopeless. Through these poems the reader will find inspiration to continue his or her race in life.

As always a book will speak to some more than others, but we must keep in mind that each poem is an expression of a heart that needs to express itself.

I, myself do not claim to be a poet by any means. I write poetry as I feel inspired to do so. I have never sat at my desk and tried to think of something to write. I believe the Lord puts the thoughts in my heart and by his grace he helps me put them together in poetic form.

Some of the poems in this book were given on special occasions. Some were given at a time of loss in someone's life. Others were written at a time in history where we stand today. Poetry gives birth to various forms of expression.

I am putting my collection of poems in book form because I believe they were given to be shared with others and enjoyed.

Poetry can soothe and comfort the heart at a time of loss. It can encourage at a time of discouragement. It can inspire one to be what God intended one to be. Poems can give hope where there seems to be no hope. Poetry sometimes reaches areas in the heart where other forms of expression cannot reach.

Poetry can reach in and touch a hardened heart and make it soft. It can take a broken heart and give it hope, it can be a means to strengthen someone's faith or it can inspire someone to reach out to God, to put their trust in him.

I have entitled this book Rays of Hope seeing we are living in a time where hope seems to be lost in the chaos of everything that is happening all around us. We are living in those times the bible calls dark times, where darkness is covering the earth and gross darkness the people. It's a time when anything goes. Evil is on the rise. It's at those times that God's glory can shine brightest. His glory is expressed in different forms of expression. Poetry is one of them.

Sometimes a poem can be a spark of light in darkness. It can be the very thing that sparks a ray of hope in someone's heart.

My intention for writing this book is to touch the hearts of those who need a ray of hope to keep them going.

My prayer is that these poems will minister to you, the reader.

I have enjoyed poetry ever since I can remember. Poetry always has a way of brightening up my day. I never thought I would one day write it in hope of reaching the hearts of those who need a little encouragement.

One poem is very special to me. It was given to me at the time of my daughter-in-laws pregnancy. It describes how God was molding and putting my granddaughter together in her mother's womb. Another one is about the cry of the lost. It's about the cry of the hurting and lost, those shunned by society. It's a cry that many times falls on deaf ears but is loud and clear to the Lord. God hears the cry of hurting people, even when others can't hear it.

Another poem is about the fingerprints of God. It speaks of how God's fingerprints can be seen in everything he created. God left fingerprints in his creation all around us and no one can deny their existence.

Rays of Hope is an expression of God's love and care for us. I believe this book will be an inspiration to you and will bring hope where hope has been lost and strength where strength is needed.

Fingerprints of God

*The heavens declare the glory of God; and the firmament shows
His handiwork. Psalm 19:1*

The summer sky at times is brilliantly lit up with millions of stars. One
stands in awe of the awesomeness of God's creation and the vastness of the
universe. It's a display of the fingerprints of God.

One time in particular comes to mind. We were in a town called Marfa,
Texas which is famous for the Marfa lights. It is said that if you look out
in a certain direction on a clear night that you can see lights appear and
disappear.

Like everyone else who visits Marfa, we went to see the Marfa lights. I
wasn't as impressed with the lights as I was with the summer sky. The
summer sky was lit up with millions and millions of dancing stars sparkling
like diamonds in the sky. The Milky Way was so immense and awesome, a
glorious sight to behold. I swear one could almost reach up and touch the
stars. I stood in awe as I marveled at the greatness of our God. It's not
every night one gets to witness God's handiwork in the sky.

How can anyone deny the existence of God? He is everywhere we look. He
is in everything we see. His fingerprints are on all of his creation.

For since the creation of the world His invisible attributes are clearly seen, being understood by the things that are made, even his eternal power and Godhead, so that they are without excuse. Romans 1:20

The world is such a beautiful place. There had to be a master mind behind its creation. It didn't just happen out of nothing. Everywhere we look we see the fingerprints of God. The word of God says God spoke the worlds into existence and he upholds them with the word of his power. The bible tells us that since the beginning of creation the attributes of God are clearly understood by the things that are made or the things we can see.

Our family lives part of the year in the Ozarks. Our home is situated on a hill surrounded by God's handiwork. Every room in my home has a magnificent view of the Ozarks. Every season has its own beauty. In the spring, flowering plants of different varieties and color are in bloom everywhere, trees are sprouting new leaves and birds are singing their praises to their maker. A small creek runs at the bottom of the hill. It doesn't carry much water and it doesn't look like much. But when it rains, water gushes down the rocks and into the creek. In a matter of hours it can transform a small creek into a raging river. There's a natural waterfall formed on the rocks behind my home every time it rains. As the water rushes over the rocks it produces the sound of a small waterfall. I like to sit out on the patio and enjoy the cool evenings and the beauty all around me. It seems that time stands still and peace just fills the air.

There is so much natural beauty in our world. In the summer time, the nights light up with fireflies. We have our own fireworks on Independence Day. Fireflies light up the darkness like a million sparkling lights among the trees. As we were driving up to our home the other night, we could see the green grass glistening with fireflies. It was an amazing sight to behold. Everything is green and full of life.

Fall is an awesome time of year in the Ozarks. I believe there is every color of tree you can imagine. We have beautiful purple, orange, yellow and red leaves everywhere. I enjoy watching the leaves come cascading down from the trees. It is a beautiful place for a painter. I can't help but think that our God is the greatest painter of all on the canvas of life.

Winter is a beautiful time of year. When it snows, the trees and hillside glisten with snow like a million crystals sparkling in the sun. It has a beauty all its own. I like to see the ice that forms on the rocks and the icicles that hang from them. It makes the hillside appear as a crystal, winter wonderland.

Branson is surrounded by lakes, which add to the beauty of the landscape. It is so peaceful there. It seems that time moves slower. Unlike the traffic in Branson, there's no hustling and bustling of traffic jams or screaming sirens out here in the country. We're surrounded by God's handiwork.

As I behold the beauty of God's creation all around me, I can't help but see the fingerprints of God as I stand in awe of his greatness. I see God's handiwork in his creation of humanity. We are so different and yet we're so alike, created in the image of God. The bible says we are fearfully and wonderfully made. Each one of us is unique. That's why we can never succeed at being anyone else. God made me unique and he made you unique. I can't be you and you can't be me. Each one has a unique portion of God's creative ability on the inside. God created you with a special plan for your life unlike any other. The Bible tells us in Jeremiah 29:11 that God's thoughts toward us are thoughts of peace and not of evil, to give us a future and a hope. His thoughts are good thoughts toward us.

We are living in the age of technology. One doesn't even have to understand it to use it, to benefit from it. How did we ever make it without cell phones? How did teenagers survive without texting? How did we exist without the computer and the World Wide Web?

In America we are blessed to be a land of all races. Each race is unique in how God created it and yet we all benefit from one another. Every race has something to offer to the rest of humanity. God made us diverse. Color makes the human race beautiful. As God's creation created in his image, we are all alike. We were created by the same creator with diversities of gifts and talents to bless one another. God likes variety.

Unbelieving men have tried to make us believe there is no God. They have tried to prove it in many ways. They have tried to make us believe that we have come from apes. That there was a big bang and when all the dust settled, bang, there was the earth with all creation in it. They haven't been successful at proving it, because God's fingerprints cannot be erased. They cannot be denied. God's fingerprints are unique. He left plenty of them for all eternity.

I believe it's more intelligent to believe the creation story than to believe we have evolved out of nothing. I've been around for awhile and I haven't evolved into anything else. I am still me. I'm still the person God created me to be, unique. I haven't seen anyone else evolve into anything else either, which causes me to believe the word of God above the theory of evolution.

God's fingerprints are in the rocks, in the seas, in the desert, in the mountains, in the heavens above and in all the earth. His likeness can be seen in you and me as we were wonderfully and fearfully made in his image, intelligent human beings.

Who is like unto our God? Who has spread forth the heavens and created the earth to be inhabited? We cannot understand his infinite wisdom, but he has allowed us to have a small portion of it. He has put a little bit of himself in each one of us and together we form a bigger picture of God.

> The works of God are great, studied by all who have pleasure in
> them. Psalm 111:2

Poem

Fingerprints of God

Oh Lord!

When I look into the sky at night,

I wonder at the awesomeness of such splendor up above.

Here below, I marvel at the majestic mountains, the mighty rivers, the valleys and the seas.

I see the greatness of your majesty.

I see the beauty of your love.

The fingerprints of God are in everything I see.

I can only stand and marvel, at the greatness all around me.

When I contemplate, how you created the whole human race,

I can't help but stand in awe of your amazing grace.

Fingerprints of mercy, fingerprints of grace

Fingerprints of love are left in every place.

I see the fingerprints of God in your creativity.

In the little bit of you, that was placed inside of me.

Beyond myself, I see your grace and your ability.

I see it working on the inside of me.

Leaving behind, fingerprints of God for everyone to see

To My Unborn Grandchild

I wrote this poem about my granddaughter Bobbie while she was still in her mother's womb. At the time I didn't know the baby would be a girl. It's exciting to know that God knows everything about us from the very beginning of conception and at times lets us in on what he's doing.

Bobbie is a beautiful ten years old at the time of this writing.

Children are a special gift from God. They are so innocent and so vulnerable. They are beautiful. It's amazing to think that God would entrust us with such a precious gift. A baby can make a grown person throw all caution to the wind and act like a child, unconcerned about what anyone thinks. I thank God that he gave such a gift to us so we could enjoy. Children are such a blessing.

I believe that God uses children to accomplish his plan and purpose. Children are so trusting. They will believe anything that is told them. We have a great responsibility to teach these children not only in word but also in our actions. Children not only believe what they hear, they are great at imitating what they see. It's our responsibility to walk upright before them and leave a good example for them to follow.

If we can change a child we can change a generation. If we can change a generation we can change our nation. If we can change our nation we can change the world.

I've seen generation upon generation lost because they weren't taught the word of God or trained to be doers of the word. I'm talking about children brought up in church. These children have grown up to be youth that rebel against authority, babies having babies. The word of God instructs us to train up a child in the way he should go.

> Proverbs 22:6 train up a child in the way he should go, and when
> he is old he will not depart from it.

Many times we find ourselves training our children in the way they shouldn't go, telling them they shouldn't do this or that but never explaining to them why. Training involves much more than telling them what not to do. If we bring them up trained in the word of God, the word of God will be their guiding light to guide them through life. They will understand why they are instructed to stay away from certain things and will gain the strength to resist temptation when it comes.

Our children are growing up in a much different world than the one we grew up in. Temptation to sin is greater as is the temptation to follow the crowd.

Today we live in a world where anything goes. Our children are faced with temptations we weren't faced with. Our children and grandchildren are growing up in a selfish world. We must instruct them and bring them up in the love and admonition of the Lord so that they learn how to esteem one another.

Children brought up in the love of God learn to prefer others. They learn to value friendships and they learn to respect what belongs to others.
If all children learned these things we wouldn't have all the bullying we see today which has caused many young people to take their own life.
We as parents and grandparents have a great responsibility before God.

> *Do not withhold correction from the child, for if you beat him with a rod, he will not die. You shall beat him with a rod, and deliver his soul from hell. Proverbs 23:13-14*

This is not talking about child beating. It is talking about the rod of correction. Children come equipped with padding on the back side for a reason. A child needs to know parents mean what they say. If he or she doesn't do what he or she is told, there will be consequences to those actions.

Training involves so much more than discipline alone. There's the correction of wrongs, to keep them on the right track and there's discipline for disobedience. Training is following through by keeping one's word about what we say we are going to do and doing it. Children need to be disciplined in a spirit of love, tenderness and concern.

The bible tells us that we are fearfully and wonderfully made in the image of God. God corrects us when we do wrong and he disciplines us. He expects us to do the same with our children.

> *I will praise you, for I am fearfully and wonderfully made: marvelous are your works, and that my soul knows very well. My frame was not hidden from you, when I was made in secret, and skillfully wrought in the lowest parts of the earth. Your eyes saw my substance, being yet unformed; and in your book they all were written, the days fashioned for me, when as yet there was none of them. Psalm 139:14-16*

It's wonderful to know that God took so much care in fashioning each one of us. He paid attention to every minute detail. God knows everything about us. There is nothing hidden from him.

I am grateful to the Lord because he has afforded me the opportunity to see my granddaughter grow and to be a small part of her life. I see in her a sweet and tender spirit.

We are careful to walk upright before her and our other grandchildren and to be examples they can follow. The plan for her life has already been laid out. Day by day her life is being patterned after something or someone. It's our responsibility to see that her life is patterned after the Lord. When she grows up, she will be able to identify with Christ and not with the world.

My prayer for her is that she will be spared the heartache many young people are going through today. Rebellion is running rampant in our society. Our young people think it's cool to do what everyone else is doing with no thought of the consequences, no thought that many of the cool things they are doing today may be the heartache of tomorrow and regret of things they cannot change.

Poem

To My Unborn Grandchild

Though you're very tiny and yet cannot be seen,

I lift you up in prayer before the King of kings.

I know he's working in you, making all the intricate parts.

He's delicately fashioning you, his greatest work of art.

The pretty eyes, the tiny mouth, and a perfect nose,

He's even counting out ten fingers and ten toes.

He's knitting you together inside your mother's womb.

You're bringing joy to many, as they watch you bloom.

He's placing in you, everything you will ever need,

His love, his joy, his peace in the form of a seed

The blueprint for your life has already been laid.

His workmanship is marvelous,

You are fearfully and wonderfully made.

He's putting you together, tiny part by tiny part.

The plan for your life, he has placed within your heart.

How great are his works! How great are his plans!

Even before you're born, he holds you in his hands.

Already in your parent's heart, there is a special place,

There's a love and caring and a longing to see your face.

God's works are marvelous and sought out.

You're one of his greater works, of that there is no doubt.

Be blessed my child as you grow

Grandma loves you, this I know.

To my Great grandchild

I have several grandchildren. Each one is unique and wonderful.

My great granddaughter Analiyah was born with a heart defect. When she was three months old she went through open heart surgery. She was so tiny and delicate at three months of age.

Lots of prayer went out for her. The hours of waiting dragged on as we waited in that waiting room for her to come out of surgery. We waited for what seemed like ages. When the surgeon finally came out and told us the surgery was over, we were all anxious to see her. After some time we finally got to go into the ICU. She had so many tubes attached to her we could barely see her. She looked so delicate and fragile. She began to amend as babies do and we were able to hold her in our arms and feed her.

One day as I entered her room I noticed her little feet and tummy were swollen. I asked the nurse about it, she said it was normal. Me, being a nurse myself, didn't agree with her. She began to have difficulty breathing. The doctor was finally called. She was taken back into surgery. Her lung had been punctured while putting in an IV. Here we were back to square one, waiting anxiously again

The surgeon comes out one more time to tell us all had gone well and we could see her shortly.

I'd think about what she must have been going through. It hurt to see her so tiny and unable to tell anyone about the pain she was feeling. I felt bad because we couldn't hold her and cuddle her like babies like to be held. I asked God to send angels to watch over her and to comfort her when she cried and a poem came out of it.

At this writing she is three years old. She is a very healthy baby and very strong. To look at her one would never think she had been through so much.

I believe the angels of God were watching over her. I know the Lord brought her through the surgeries because he has a special plan for her life just as he has for each and every one of us.

Poem

To My Great Grandchild Analiyah

You are such a brave little baby you've gone through so much.

Angels took their stand as the battle was fought.

God brought you through victoriously because there's something special in you.

In the future he has something planned that only you can do.

As you went through the surgeries, he held you in his hand and assigned angels to watch over you.

They protected you and made sure no harm would come to you.

At the tiniest little cry, they would take you in their arms and sing sweet lullabies.

When you dosed off to sleep, they gently laid you down, placing little butterfly kisses as you made a little frown.

Listen!

You can almost hear the brush of angel's wings as they gently flutter by.

They are ready to comfort you at the slightest little cry.

You are special and God has a plan for you, of something great and mighty that only you can do.

You are my special angel sent from God above known to all of us as a bundle of love.

My Granddaughter Tiggy

Jhaielynn Antigone is this sweet vibrant little girl. She has always had a very sweet spirit about her. At this writing she just celebrated her fourth birthday.

She is a little dreamer. My oldest granddaughter got married in March and Antigone was so excited she could hardly contain herself. She thought she was watching a real princess. She hasn't stopped asking when she can be a princess and wear the beautiful gown too.

When Antigone watches a movie she pretends she is an actor in the movie. She watched Tangled and now she thinks the fireworks on the fourth of July represent her birthday. Her birthday is on the fifth of July.

I remember when Antigone was a little baby she would just melt in my arms and give real hugs. Her personality is going to take her a long ways. God has a special plan for her life.

I wrote this poem for her because she is one of my special angels. I have five little girls under the age of four. All of them are angels in my eyes.

Poem

To My Great granddaughter Tiggy

When I look into your eyes I see such a tender heart.

Innocence and beauty have characterized you from the start.

I recall your precious baby hugs as you'd melt into my arms.

Now you're such a dainty little girl so full of love and charm.

I pray that as you travel down life's road, nothing in this world will ever cause you any harm.

God sent special angels to watch over you.

Angels to protect and keep you safe in everything you do.

Angels on assignment are watching over you, stationed all around you in such splendid array, watching every move you make throughout each day.

One day you will grow up to be that princess you've always wanted to be, although in our eyes you are already that princess because that is what we see.

The Cry of the Lost

And he said to them, "Go into all the world and preach the gospel to every creature. Mark 16:15

Jesus gave us what is called the great commission before he left. He wants every human being to be saved. He doesn't want anyone to miss the opportunity of knowing him. After all, the price he paid for our salvation was a great price.

It took the laying down of his life for us, while we were yet sinners. There was much pain and suffering that went along with it. He suffered the pain of rejection, he was stripped of his garments, his side was pierced, he was beaten numerous times, then nailed to a cross and left to die. He never opened his mouth. He bore the pain and shame for our transgressions. He took your place and my place on the cross. We were the sinners. We deserved to die, not him. He paid a debt he did not owe so that you and I could go free from the debt we owed.

There was no way we could pay the debt. No human being nor religion could save us. We couldn't save ourselves. I think back to a time when I didn't know the Lord and I remember saying I was going to make changes in my life but I didn't have the ability to carry through with it. I failed time and time again. I couldn't do it in my own strength. I needed the grace of God. I needed a Savior.

One would think that every person in America would have heard the gospel at least once. But there are still many who have never heard. There are People on the streets of our cities who have never heard the gospel. There are people who are suffering in their own little world; People who have lost all hope. Many people are unable to see a way out of their situation. Many have been indoctrinated in a religion without Christ and with no power.

There wasn't anyone to tell me about Jesus in all the years I was growing up. I didn't know there was a different form of music. I had never seen a Christian bookstore. When we're in the world system we are truly blind. Unless someone tells us about the Lord, there's a possibility we could be lost for eternity. It's our responsibility to tell the lost about Jesus.

The apostle Paul was a man who was brought up as a Pharisee. He was taught by the best teachers of his day, but he didn't know the Lord. One day while travelling on the Damascus road he saw a great light from heaven above the brightness of the sun and he was knocked to the ground. The Lord spoke to him.

> `And when we all had fallen to the ground, I heard a voice speaking to me in the Hebrew language, Saul, Saul, why are you persecuting me? It is hard for you to kick against the goads' "so I said, who are you Lord?' And he said, `I am Jesus whom you are persecuting. But rise and stand on your feet; for I have appeared to you for this purpose, to make you a minister and a witness both of the things which you have seen and of the things which I will reveal to you. `I will deliver you from the Jewish people, as well as from the Gentiles, to whom I now send you. "To open their eyes in order to turn them from darkness to light, and from the power of Satan to God, that they may receive forgiveness of sins and an inheritance among those who are sanctified by faith in me.' Acts 26:14-18

The apostle Paul was given instructions on what he was to do. From that day forward, the apostle Paul never went back to his religion. He began to minister to anyone who would listen because the message was urgent.

There are many people sitting in darkness with no direction in life, with no goals. They are the homeless of our cities, the drug addict on the street, the prostitute trying to make a living for her family, the abused and unwanted. They are the children who are being trafficked. They need someone to tell them there is better way, someone who can look beyond the outward appearance and see the soul of a human being crying out for help.

I heard of a man who decided to go homeless for a week to see how homeless people live. It's amazing that after a few days living as a homeless person he discovered that they are real people with a soul and a spirit just like us. They have problems all their own. Many times we have to get down on their level before we can relate to them and the things they are going through. Jesus came down on our level so that he could take us up on his. Many times we look down on those who are less fortunate than us. In God's eyes their soul is just as precious as ours.

The only thing we are waiting for to usher in the return of the lord, is the gospel being preached as a witness to all nations. God patiently waits for us to get our act together. He is waiting for the church to obey the great commission "go." He hears the cries of the lost. He sees their pain. He needs people who will go and tell them, there is a way, there is hope. They can come out of their situation. They don't have to live the way they are living.

Is there anyone out there hearing the cry of the lost? Or have we also turned deaf ears to their cries?

If the Lord hadn't come to save us, we would all be doomed. The Lord is depending upon you and me to go forth and tell the world that God is no longer holding their sins against them. We must tell them God is a good God and he will forgive them of all of their sins if they repent and put their trust in him. We must tell them the price has been paid, the prison doors are open. They are free to go now.

How many people today are living in a prison they have created? How many people are waiting for someone to give them hope, someone who will show them the way of escape?

How many people are willing to go out into the highways and byways and compel them to come into God's kingdom? God rejects no one who comes to him with a sincere and repentant heart. God is longsuffering and waits with open arms for all to come to him. God never turns anyone away.

Poem

The Cry of the Lost

There are cries in the night, that fall on deaf ears.

Hurting hearts crying out, their pillow soaked with tears.

In the daytime their appearance is courageous and strong.

When alone, they know that everything is wrong.

They have no one to turn to, no one who cares,

They have no hope of a better tomorrow.

Their nights are filled with fears.

What is a soul worth?

Does anyone know the cost?

Why isn't anyone hearing the cry of the lost?

Who is going to tell them, their life is precious and dear?

Who is going to rescue those souls?

Does anyone care?

The days as we know them are approaching an end.

From heaven, the cry goes out, whom shall I send?

Is anyone out there who has ears to hear, the cry of the lost as the end draws near?

Where are they, the hearts of mercy, compassion and love?

Who can hear the heart cry of the Father above?

Who will go and demonstrate his love?

Jesus said Go. The command is clear.

Every human soul to the Father is dear.

If we cannot hear, the cry of the lost, we can never understand Calvary's cost.

I asked to see the Lord

Have you ever desired to see the Lord? Have you ever desired just to bask in his glory and remain in his presence? We live in a world that is governed by the five senses, we want to see and feel everything. As Christians we are required to walk by faith and not by sight. I believe every one of us has at one time or another cried out to God and said *I want to see you*. Moses at one time said to the Lord, *show me your glory*.

This poem came to me back in the year 2000 while we were Pastors in a church in Big Spring, Texas. One night during a prayer service, the glory came in like a cloud and the presence of the Lord was so strong, there was a tangible anointing. An awesome presence of the Lord was in that place. God's peace entered that room like a soft blanket falling over us. At the moment it seemed like I could reach out and touch him. I cried out, *Lord, I want to see you*.

I wasn't prepared for what I was going to see next. I wasn't prepared for what the Lord was about to show me. He showed me what he wanted me to see. Many times when we ask the Lord for something it doesn't come to us the way we think it should.

I didn't see the Lord in all of his glory. That's what I wanted to see. I didn't see him seated at the right hand of God; I didn't see him ascending in glory into heaven. Instead I saw Jesus as he hung on the cross, torn and bleeding and in so much agony. It seemed to me that I was seeing it in 3D.

I remember the feelings of love for him that washed over me. I wanted to fall at his feet weeping and hugging his feet wiping them with my tears as the woman in the bible had done. I wanted to fall at his feet and repent of the pain I had caused him. At that moment I recognized the sinfulness of man as the cause of all his suffering. I recognized my own sin that sent him to Calvary to pay the price I could not pay.

I felt so humbled that my King would come down from heaven to die for me, a sinner. I literally fell at his feet and wept. I know how the woman felt; who washed his feet with her tears and wiped them with her hair. She must have been overcome with love.

The crucifixion of the Lord, that day became a reality I will never forget. That picture is forever engraved in my heart. It has caused me to appreciate what he has done for me more than I ever had before. It helped me see the reality of the price Jesus paid for me. Many of us take for granted what he did for us. We're saved. We don't have to worry about going to Hell when we die. We soon forget what brought us to the cross.

The crucifixion wasn't easy. The pain was real. The suffering was real. The nails that pierced his hands and feet were real. The crown of thorns they placed upon his brow piercing his brow and causing tremendous pain was real. He was led like a sheep to the slaughter and he didn't open his mouth. The blood he shed was real blood and he did it for you and me. He did it to pave the way so that you and I could be set free. The road to freedom is paved with blood. No wonder folks throughout the ages have sung about the precious blood of Jesus. It was the only thing that could set the captives free. It's the only thing that could erase our sin and cleanse us and make us new creatures in him. Our God is an awesome God.

I Asked to see the Lord

I asked to see the Lord, expecting to see his glory.

Instead I saw a close up of the crucifixion story.

There stood the cross before me.

It appeared to be in 3-D!

A real human body hung on Calvary's tree.

It was real blood that day that flowed for you and me.

I saw the pain, the suffering, the grief and the shame,

I humbly fell before him on my knees.

I knew I was to blame!

I said, my lord I'm sorry,

I've never seen you this way.

I thought I'd see your glory

Instead I saw your shame.

I will never forget this moment, how much it means to me.

I saw the very thing, you wanted me to see.

It wasn't just a story.

It's as real as can be.

You really did pay the price for all humanity.

The Shattered Vase

We as human beings go through many tests and trials. Many times the things we've gone through leave behind scars of pain, humiliation and regret.

My heart goes out to those who have been abused and those who feel rejected. Many times when we suffer abuse of any kind, whether it be physical or sexual abuse, it leaves behind a feeling of unworthiness. We feel like maybe we were to blame for what happened to us. We feel like everyone is judging us unworthy but in reality we have judged ourselves. There are many regrets of past mistakes we live with. Regret has a voice and that voice asks the question, what if? There are many "what ifs" in everyone's life.

We can't go back and change any of it. The bible tells us we are to forget the things that are behind. It's not easy to forget the past, but it's not impossible.
The Lord helps us forget if we put our trust in him. We can never take hold of the future if we keep holding on to our past mistakes. There is nothing you or I can do to change the past. If we want to go on with life we have to trade the past for the future.

Yes the pain of abuse is real, I don't belittle that. I know what it's like to live with regret, to wish things could have been different. The poem I wrote is about me. I was a shattered vase. I was a mess. I spent years listening to the voice of regret. I didn't think I could get over it. It took the love of God to put me back together again. It didn't happen overnight. It took a lot of love and patience. It took the renewing of my mind before I could see myself as God sees me. I had to quit identifying with the past.

I had to learn to trust the Lord. I had to learn to forgive myself and forgive the person who wronged me. I had to learn to believe that God loves me. I had to learn to believe that God so loved me, that he gave his only begotten son to die for me, so that I could be made the righteousness of God in him. He took my unrighteousness and gave me his righteousness. He made me worthy and he made you worthy. God did not send his son into the world to condemn the world but that the world through him might be saved, according to the gospel of John, John 3:16-17.

Whatever pain you have suffered, he is able to erase the scars of the past and give you a beautiful future. Many times it's hard to believe that God loves us because we have judged our self as unworthy of his love. It's difficult for us because we find it hard to love or forgive ourselves; we find it hard to believe God can forgive us, love us and help us start over.

Life isn't always fair. Many times it throws us a hard blow. Some people never recover. Many people continue to live with the pain of the past. Many people take the pain and regret of the past to the grave.

In sharing this poem I have in mind all of you out there who feel unworthy and rejected. My desire is to help you see yourself as God sees you. I want you to know that you can find your true worth in Christ. You are a valuable human being. God created you with potential to be somebody.

I can say from experience that God is able to transform your life and cause all things to work together for your good. I think of how gently and tenderly God worked with me. I think of how he took my broken life and put it back together again. He takes those shattered vases and makes them vessels of great value. What great love the father has for his creation!

What great love Jesus has for us, that he would come down from his place of glory and take on a human form in order to make it possible to relate to the pain and suffering we are going through.

Don't allow your past to identify who you are. Turn a deaf ear to the voice of regret. Change the way you see yourself and start seeing yourself as God sees you. Your true value is found in him.
Choose not to be a victim of your past.

The Shattered Vase

There once was a shattered vase, discarded by everyone.

Broken and battered, the damage had been done.

One day God walked through the rubbish, to see what he could find.

To see what was left of what sin had left behind.

He saw the shattered vase, pieces scattered everywhere.

He picked them up so gently, with tender loving care.

As he spread them out before him, he saw rejection, fear. Despair.

Sin left nothing good. It was so unfair!

He took them to his son and began to lay them out.

Abuse, insecurities, addictions, the pieces were all there.

Moved with such compassion! Jesus began to speak, *"lo I come to do thy will oh God, whatever the cost may be."*

"I will go down to earth and set humanity free."

A body, God prepared for him. He did it all for me, and sent him down to die on Calvary's tree.

Bleeding on the cross that day, he hung between heaven and earth.

The road was being paved with blood, so we could have new birth.

I'm so grateful for God's compassion and how Jesus loved me so.

I'll never forget the words, of the great commission, go!

Out there are many shattered vases, many broken reeds.

Sin and shame has taken its toll, but we have what they need.

I can never forget where I came from. I was that shattered vase.

To the world around me, I was an impossible case.

But Jesus came and saved me, through a demonstration of his love.

The greatest gift one can receive is Jesus, God's gift from up above.

When You Need Strength

Have you ever had one of those days, when it seems like you're not going to make it through the day? You wake up with the feeling like, it would be better to go back to sleep and wake up again. You feel like you don't even have the strength to get out of bed. Maybe you're going through one of those days as you read this book. It seems like the last thread of strength is gone. That every move you make takes every ounce of energy you have left. Everything that can go wrong is going wrong. You wish you could just crawl back into bed and start over. Those are times when we have to lean on someone who is stronger than our self, a power greater than ourselves.

> I can do all things through Christ which strengthened me.
> Philippians 4:13

> 2 Corinthians 12:9 says: And he said to me, "My grace is sufficient for you, for my strength is made perfect in weakness."

When we are weak, then we are strong, because that's when God's grace goes to work for us. God's grace is God's ability working in us to help us do what we cannot do in our own strength.

God will always make a way for us, even when there seems to be no way. Even when we can't see how he is going to do it. We just have to trust him. He said he would never leave us nor forsake us. He said those who put their trust in him will never be disappointed.

You might feel alone, but you are never alone. You might feel like nobody cares, but God cares. Maybe you're feeling like your problems will never go away. With the Lord on your side you can make it through any problem. No matter how big your problem seems today, tomorrow it won't seem quite as big. God is bigger than your problem. When you have the assurance that you're not going through that trial alone, it gives you the strength you need to make it through and come out victorious on the other side.

How you view your problem makes all the difference in the outcome of your situation. If you see defeat you have already defeated yourself. If you think you can't, you can't. If you see yourself as the over comer, you will overcome any situation that comes your way. If you see yourself victorious, you will come out victorious.

Many times our problems appear bigger according to how we view our problems. If we dwell on the problem instead of the answer we will always find ourselves defeated. When we focus on the problem, it becomes bigger than our God. We need to take our eyes off the problem and get them on Jesus. God is bigger than any problem we will ever face. He promised to be with us through the waters and the rivers and the fire. *Isaiah 43:2*. He is our refuge and our strength a very present help in trouble. *Psalms 46:1*. It's during those times that it seems the hardest to believe he is actually present with us in all of our troubles.

Many times I have to tell myself, there is nothing that God and I can't handle, we are a majority. As long as God is for me as he said in his word, I have nothing to be concerned about. If I roll all of my cares on him, there's nothing left for me to worry about. I didn't learn this overnight. I used to be a world class worrier, I worried about everything. I worried about worry. But as I began to read God's word and meditate on it, I began to see that I can turn my cares over to him because he cares for me. If they are too big for me, I can't handle them but he can. It's great to sleep at night without a worry knowing that God never slumbers nor sleeps, knowing God is taking care of my problems for me. It's great to know that God never leaves us nor forsakes us, that angels are watching over us.

Many times Jesus would say to his disciples fear not. He knew that fear paralyses faith and makes it inoperative. Fear is the opposite of faith, when fear comes in faith goes out.

Poem

When You Need Strength

When you need strength to get you through the day,

And your problems seem like they're never going away.

When you look outside and the sky looks grey,

Remember that the Lord will always make a way.

He never leaves you nor forsakes you, no matter what you do.

His arms are always open, waiting for you

The day will become brighter.

Your heartache cannot stay.

And you will find your problems will vanish away.

So look to Jesus when you're feeling this way.

You will find that gloom and darkness cannot stay.

God is with you he will see you through

No matter how things look, he's looking out for you.

What is a Friend?

Everyone needs a friend. Everyone needs someone whom they can confide in. Everyone needs someone that can be trusted to keep a secret. All of us need someone who will always be there for us.

A friend is one who never judges you, for the dumb things you do, someone who can overlook your mistakes, someone who can see beyond your shortcomings and love you anyway.

We all want someone to believe in us and to encourage us when we are down, one who is able to make us laugh, one who is able to lift up our spirit when we are feeling discouraged, one who always has the right thing to say at the right time.

There are certain people who cross our path, who turn out to be just the kind of people we need in our life at that particular time. The Lord is the only one who knows what we need and he brings those people across our path. The Lord has brought so many wonderful people into my life. I call them divine connections, people I can count on, people I can trust, those who sincerely care about me. The world is full of wonderful people. Sometimes it doesn't seem like it. When we hear about all the evil that is happening in our world, it seems that no one cares about anyone else. Regardless of what it looks like, there are still many caring people in our world.

God's people are wonderful people because they all have a little bit of God, a little bit of his creative power. Each person is unique in his own way. A real friend will draw out the uniqueness in a person.

You might think you have no real talent. I don't believe a person exists that has no talent. Sometimes those talents are hidden and can be brought out by just the right person. I believe we all have been given certain gifts and talents. I believe we all have something that someone needs. A true friend always encourages you to be your very best and helps you believe in yourself.

A friend is an encourager. He or she will encourage you when you are feeling down. A friend will weep with you when you feel like weeping. He or she will rejoice with you when you are happy. A friend will always say to you, "you can do it."

We have a friend like that in the Lord. The bible tells us there is a friend that sticks closer than a brother. That is close. He will never leave you. He will never forsake you. He is the only friend you can count on to be there every time you need him. He never slumbers nor sleeps. He is there in the darkest hour of your night. He is the only friend who knows everything about you and loves you just the same. God loves you in spite of you.

There is one thing you can always count on; he believes in you, he knows your potential, he knows your ability and he knows your inabilities. He knows your strengths and he knows your weakness. He placed inside of you everything you will ever need to accomplish your goals in life and to see your dreams realized.

We just don't dream enough. The reason people don't dream enough is because they don't think they have the ability to accomplish their dreams. A dream is what motivates us to reach for bigger and better things in life. God and you are a majority. In him you can do all things.

I never thought I could accomplish anything, because I didn't believe in myself. God has brought me to a place where I believe now there is nothing I can't do, if I put my trust in him.

If you are a young person, don't wait till you're old to accomplish your goals. If you're an older person don't give up on your dreams. You can still dream and you can still see the realization of those dreams. It's not a matter of whether you are young or old. It's a matter of whether you fulfill your destiny regardless of your age.

Many men in the bible were not used of God until they were seventy or eighty years of age, yet they did great things for God. God didn't think they were over the hill. When you reach the top of the hill it's time to pick up speed, not time to quit.

Many times all it takes is a friend that believes in you. Jesus is that kind of friend.

Poem

What is a friend?

A friend is someone you can count on when everyone else is gone.

Someone you can tell everything to.

A friend is someone who doesn't judge you for the dumb things that you do.

A friend is someone who believes in you when no one seems to care.

When you need someone to talk to,

A friend is always there.

A friend believes in you when you can't believe in yourself.

A friend encourages you to be everything you can be.

The Lord brings certain people across your path.

No matter what you're going through, he or she can always make you laugh.

Friends are never forgotten, no matter how far apart.

A friend is a friend forever, cherished in the heart.

Don't be Afraid

At the time of this writing we are seeing many things taking place in our world that can produce fear. We are living in perilous times. Our economy is unstable. Many are losing their jobs in which they have trusted. Many established companies are closing their doors. The future looks bleak. The enemy uses the things that are seen to create fear in individuals.

We are living in what the bible calls *the last days*. Just watching the evening news can be disturbing. It seems like evil is all around us. Thank God we have the promise that he will keep us from the evil one.

It's easy to let fear come in when we are seeing an increase in earth quakes and tornadoes and hurricanes that destroy, when everything that can be shaken is being shaken.

At this writing Japan just experienced a major devastating earthquake and tsunami. It was a very frightening and devastating experience for the people of Japan.

> The bible says God has not given us a spirit of fear; but of power, and of love and of a sound mind. 2 Timothy 1:7

As Christians we have nothing to fear. We can look to the future with great expectation, knowing that God will take care of us.

The bible says when these things begin to happen, look up and lift up your head, because your redemption draws near Luke 21:28. Don't look around at the circumstances; don't listen to what the media is saying. We have a promise of a great future. Lift up your head, look up!

The things we are seeing have been prophesied. It's time for us to take inventory of where we stand with the Lord. We want to be ready to escape the things that are coming on the earth and to stand before the Lord.

Are you ready?

> "Watch therefore, and pray always, that you may be counted worthy to escape all these things that will come to pass, and to stand before the son of man." Luke 21:36

The bible warns us that the end is going to come as a snare upon all them that dwell on the face of the whole earth. It also instructs us as to what we can do to prepare ourselves and be ready so that day does not catch us by surprise. Many are going about their business, doing their own thing, unaware of what is going on around them. The day of the Lord is fast approaching; the signs are all around us. We must be alert and watching, lest we also get caught up in the cares of this world. With so many distractions all around us it's not hard to do.

The bible tells us that it will be as the days of Noah. One hundred twenty years Noah warned them of an impending flood coming to destroy the earth and every living thing, but they continued to live as if that day would never come. They ignored the warning signs, they ignored Noah's preaching

We Christians should always be ready especially as we see the day approaching.

Some of the things the Lord told us to look out for are:

> Take heed that ye be not deceived. Luke 21:8
> But when ye shall hear of wars and commotions, be not terrified; but the end is not by and by. Luke 21:9
> Nation shall rise against nation, and kingdom against kingdom. Luke 21:10
> And great earthquakes shall be in divers places, and famines, and pestilences; and fearful sights and great signs shall there be from heaven. Luke 21:11
> And then shall many be offended and betray one another, and shall hate one another. And many false prophets shall arise, and shall deceive many. And because iniquity shall abound, the love of many shall wax cold. But he that shall endure unto the end, the same shall be saved. And this gospel of the kingdom shall be preached in all the world for a witness unto all nations; and then shall the end come. Matthew 24:10-14
> But take heed to yourselves, lest your hearts be weighed down with carousing, drunkenness. And the cares of this life, and that day come upon you unexpectedly. For it will come as a snare on those who dwell on the face of the whole earth. Luke 21:34-35

Poem

Don't be Afraid

Though there be wars and rumors of war, don't be afraid.

Though there be earthquakes and chaos everywhere

Don't be afraid.

You can be assured the end is not here.

If you're watching, you will know when the time is near.

When storm clouds start to form on the horizon, becoming more intense,

Darkness is increasing and things just don't make sense,

Men's hearts failing them for the roaring of the sea,

They look around but there's no place to flee,

Don't be afraid.

It's time to look up for your redemption draws neigh.

Soon we will see Jesus coming in the clouds in the sky.

There is nothing to fear, if we watch and pray.

We will all be ready to meet him on that day.

How to Arrive at Your Destination

So many people want to get where they're going without meeting challenges along the way. Everyone is looking for a short cut. Man always wants to take the path of least resistance. What most people don't realize is that taking the path of least resistance usually takes them where they don't want to go. How many people have taken the path of least resistance and ended up somewhere they didn't intend to end up at?

There are no short cuts in life. There's no easy way to get to the place of success. Many times we find that what we think is a short cut ends up taking up more of our time and energy.

These days many vehicles have a GPS system which gives directions to arrive at your destination. One person I know set her GPS to take the route of least traffic. She didn't know that taking the route of least traffic was going to lead her all over the country side to get to her home. She did avoid traffic but it took her a hundred miles out of her way. A short cut is not always what you think it will be.

Is there a dream in your heart, is there a destination you want to arrive at? You are going to have to face the challenges that rise up to challenge you. You can't go around them. You can't go over them. You have to go through them. The only way you can face your giants is head on. The shortest way to arrive at your destination is by taking one step at a time. It takes discipline and patience. Most people don't like patience. My granddaughter says she doesn't like patience because it takes too long.

There was a time when I was working fifty miles away from home. I took different routes every day to try to find a short cut, I just wanted to get home as quick as possible after a long day. I found out that a straight line between two points is the shortest route. Sometimes I'd end up miles away from home, farther away than I wanted to go. It was so frustrating. We always get frustrated when we try to arrive at our destination by taking a short cut. Many times we end up encountering things that slow us down. We encounter giants we weren't expecting to rise up. Obstacles out of nowhere pop up that we were not expecting.

How far you want to go in life depends upon you. Are you willing to take life one step at a time? Are you willing to be patient as you wait for your dream to come to pass? How much effort are you putting into your dream? Dreams don't come to pass on their own. If you have a dream in your heart you have to put some work into it. It's not out of reach. It's a question of how much do you want it? Are you willing to make sacrifices? No dream comes to pass without sacrifice. You're going to find that sometimes the road gets rough and bumpy but you can't quit. Dreamers never quit.

The road to success is paved with discouragements, disappointments and sometimes failures before you reach your destination. Failing doesn't make you a failure. What makes you a failure is when you refuse to get up and try again.

We have to learn to face our fears head on. Anyone who has ever tried to succeed at anything has found that fear is a big giant that rises up to mock you. Fear will tell you, you can't do it. It will tell you, you don't have what it takes. Your determination for success has to be greater than your fear of failure.

It's in the trying times of our life that character is built. It's through those times that we become established in what we want, and we go after it with everything we've got.

A good character will increase your chances for success. Success is defined different for different individuals. For some it's having a successful business, for others it's fame and fortune, for others it's becoming all that they can be for the Lord. You can never have good success without good character. Character will sustain you in the hard times. Character will keep you going until you reach your destination.

Success is achieved one step at a time. It never happens overnight. It's unrealistic to think that one can achieve success over night. One thing you can be assured of, you will arrive at your destination if you don't take detours. Sometimes you may have to pull back for awhile but it's not a setback. You can always take up where you left off.

You will arrive at your destination if you become determined to stay on track. You will stay on track if you don't let distractions slow you down, if you use tests and trials as stepping stones on the way to where you're going.

You will arrive at your destination when you are determined to win. You will get there when you are determined not to let anything take you off course.

Poem

How to Arrive at Your Destination

Success is achieved one step at a time, with a dream in the heart and determination.

Success is achieved by a goal in your heart and firing up your imagination.

One step at a time, you will find,

is the shortest route to arrive there on time.

How far you want to go in life is up to you.

How you get there depends on what you do.

Never let go no matter how rough.

Never quit when the going gets tough.

The road to success is paved with discouragement and tears, learning how to get a handle on your fears.

Character is built in trying circumstances.

A good character always increases your chances.

One day those dreams and goals will no longer be an imagination.

One day you will wake up to find, you have arrived at your destination.

Disappointments

Disappointments are a part of life. None of us are going to leave earth without them. One thing we can be sure of things are going to change. Tomorrow you will see things in a different light. Disappointments are never here to stay; they are something we have to go through.

Many don't know how to handle disappointments, when their plans are interrupted, their whole day is ruined and their world falls apart. When disappointments come there's a choice to be made, we can either choose to go through them or we can choose to camp out in our disappointments. Like everything else disappointments come and go. We have to be determined when disappointments come that they are not going to disappoint us. If one dwells on the disappointments long enough discouragement will come. When discouragement comes, one just wants to give up and quit.

Disappointments weigh down the heart and make it heavy. It seems like everything that can go wrong will go wrong. We all have those days. The outcome of it is determined by how you and I respond to the situation. Those are the times that you must encourage yourself in the Lord. He will never disappoint you. He understands what you are going through even when no one else seems to understand. While you are spending time with him your disappointments disappear. Those things you thought were so important fade away in his presence. Like the dew with the morning sun, your disappointments just melt away.

Why do we become disappointed? Is it because things don't go our way? Is it because circumstances change things? Is it because our way didn't work? If our way isn't working it's time to change what we're doing. Many times we want to get different results doing the same thing.

Many times we cause our disappointments by thinking we need to be in control of every situation. I never felt freer than when I discovered that there are things I cannot change no matter what I do and those are the things I need to leave alone. The word says we are to cast all of our cares upon Him because He cares for us. If we do that and we don't take our cares back when we get through praying, they are no longer in our hands they're in his. God is well able to handle all of our situations, if we leave them with him and trust him to solve our problem.

People get disappointed and become offended. We get disappointed because someone else doesn't see it the way we do. The best that one can do is to learn to discourage disappointments, to change the things we can change and to leave the rest alone.

Why do we think we have to be in control? Maybe it's because we ourselves are insecure, maybe it's due to a lack of confidence. When we're confident in whom we are in Christ and we put our trust in him, we know he will take care of us.

Insecurity comes from lack of trust. When you trust someone, you feel secure with that person because you know he has your best interest at heart. God has your best interest at heart. You can trust him to see you through whatever situation you're going through.

Every times disappointments come there's a choice to be made. We can either let the disappointment control us or we can control the situation by knowing what we can do ourselves and what we need to turn over to the Lord.

Many times we are our own worst enemy. We allow ourselves to dwell on things that we have no control over. The Apostle Paul said we should dwell on good things.

> *Finally, brethren, whatever things are true, whatever things are noble, whatever things are just, whatever things are pure, whatever things are lovely, whatever things are of good report, if there is any virtue and if there is anything praise-worthy-meditate on these things. Philippians 4:8*

Poem

Disappointments

My heart is heavy, I feel weighed down.

I cry out to the Lord in my despair.

Lord! I feel like I'm drowning.

I don't know what to do.

In my despair I cry out to you.

I feel like I've reached the end of my rope.

And I'm barely holding on by a last thread of hope.

In the silence I hear a still small voice,

Like a gentle whisper say, I'm here.

I'm here to wrap my arms around you, to wipe away the tears.

To tell you that I love you and let you know I care.

Disappointments are not here to stay.

Like a shadow they will soon flee away.

The sun rises and shadows disappear with the dawn.

Everything looks different from here.

As the dew on the grass melts with the sun,

The pain I was feeling, now is gone.

I can meet disappointments head on and say

I'm glad my God always makes a way.

Discouraging Discouragement

I once taught a message on discouraging discouragement. The Lord gave me a statement about discouragement. He said, *if you don't discourage discouragement, it will discourage you.*

How many times have you been discouraged and instead of discouraging it you entertained it and you ended up being more discouraged. All of us are guilty of doing that.

We have to be able to recognize discouragement when it comes. Discouragement is designed to steal your joy. The bible says in the last part of *Nehemiah 8:10 the joy of the Lord is your strength.* If we have no joy, we have no strength. Have you noticed how easy it is to become discouraged? You can be joyfully singing and enjoying the day when something happens that you weren't expecting and immediately discouragement comes to steal your joy.

One thing discouragement does, it creates a desire in you to want everyone around you to feel the way you do and it upsets you if they don't. So you call up all your friends to share your discouragement. If they are true friends they will try their best to encourage you and get you out of that mood. But many times people will agree with what you're saying and everyone ends up discouraged.

There's a story in the bible that stands out to me when we talk about discouragement. That is the story of David. He and his men had gone out to war. When they returned they found their wives and children had been taken captive. There was discouragement in the camp. The men who were with David were so discouraged that they spoke of stoning David. Even though David wept like they did, he did not allow disappointment to dictate his actions. Instead he went to the Lord and encouraged himself in the Lord. Sometimes you have to encourage yourself in the Lord because there's no one else around to encourage you. While David was encouraging himself in the Lord, the Lord instructed him as to what to do. It's amazing what encouragement can do.

When David and his men followed the Lord's instructions, they pursued the enemy. They overtook them and recovered all. Notice it wasn't till they encouraged themselves and obeyed the Lord that they were able to overtake the enemy and recover all. Instead of the enemy pursuing them they pursued the enemy.

You have an enemy who would like nothing more than to kill, steal and destroy you. When we allow our self to become discouraged it opens the door to the enemy to pursue us and destroy us. If the enemy can keep you discouraged, he can keep you defeated. People are not your enemy, the devil is.

Another thing the Lord showed me was that when we make a decision in a time of discouragement, it will always be the wrong decision. Many times when we feel discouraged, we want change and we want it now. We want things to be different. So we make hasty decisions.

To become discouraged is to lose all courage. When we lose our courage, we also lose our confidence. When we lose our confidence discouragement turns into despair. When we despair, we lose hope.

The Bible tells us that Moses, the great man of God was leading the children of Israel in the wilderness. While leading the children of Israel through the wilderness, they came to a place where there was no water. The Lord told Moses to speak to the rock so that water would come out of the rock. Moses struck the rock. The Bible tells us that Moses was disappointed with the people. He made a decision in a time of discouragement and he was not able to enter the Promised Land the Lord had promised them. He was discouraged with the children of Israel because all they did was murmur and complain. Can you imagine being with a murmuring and complaining people 24/7 for forty years. I believe I would have gotten discouraged myself. Most likely it would have happened a lot sooner than it did with Moses.

It's easy to become discouraged when you're around people who are discouraged. One has to be stronger in order to pick up the other. Weak people pull one another down. You've heard the saying, misery loves company. I would like to add that discouragement is a cousin to misery.

One has to be determined to be an over comer in every situation for discouragement not to get one down and lead one into making decisions one will later regret. We all get tired of where we're at and would like to see change but the time for change is not always now.

> My brethren, count it all joy when you fall into various trials,
> knowing that the testing of your faith produces patience. But
> let patience have its perfect work, that you may be perfect and
> complete lacking nothing. James 1:2-4

Patience helps us maintain stability. When we're patient even in times of trials, it helps us maintain the peace of God that passes all understanding. We may not understand why these things are happening to us but we can be at peace knowing that God is for us and he will see us through the tough times in our life. We can use patience as a stepping stone on the way to where we're going and we will never make the wrong decision if we follow after peace.

Poem

Discouraging, discouragement

You must discourage discouragement before it discourages you.

Discouragement gets you to the place where confusion enters in.

You begin to believe that you cannot win.

You struggle with indecision.

Your mind is in confusion.

You begin to think that there is no solution.

Encourage yourself in the Lord and you will see, discouragement that has been, will begin to flee.

As discouragement flees, the solution becomes clear.

It has always been there but was covered by fear.

Clouds of discouragement will soon flee away.

While you're trusting in him, discouragement can't stay.

There is a solution to every trial you face.

If you take your focus off the problem and turn a deaf ear to what discouragement says, you'll find the answer to your problem is found in God's amazing grace.

A Song within my Heart

And do not be drunk with wine, in which is dissipation; but be filled with the Spirit, speaking to one another in psalms and hymns and spiritual songs, singing and making melody in your heart to the Lord. Ephesians 5:18-19

I believe God puts a song in every heart. Some people say, "I can't sing." God says we can make melody in our heart and we can make a joyful noise.

I believe that a melody in one's heart keeps the heart at peace and the mind on the Lord. There is a song in your heart but many times that song is drowned out by the tests and trials of life. It has to be resurrected so that no matter what you're going through, you can choose to make melody in your heart to the Lord. It doesn't even have to be a beautiful melody. The bible tells us to make a joyful noise to the Lord. Who's to say that by the time it reaches the throne room of God that it is not transformed into a beautiful melody.

When we become Christians, we have something to be joyful about. We have a hope that anchors our soul. We have a peace that passes understanding, and we have a future. God has done great things for us. He has showered his abundant love upon us.

He has given us grace to see us through the tough times of our life. When we miss it he is merciful and forgives us. Not only does he forgive us, but he cleanses us from all unrighteousness and puts us back in right standing with himself as if we never sinned.

Sometimes the song may be a song of praise unto God, for all the great things he has done for us. Sometimes it's a song of adoration for the one who saved us. Sometimes it may be a quiet song you sing in your heart.

God delights in the praises of his people. He delights in them so much that the bible says, he inhabits the praises of his people. He comes and dwells among our praises. Music has the ability of bringing down the presence of God. How can we not have a happy heart being in the very presence of God?

A song makes the heart merry. Melody in the heart makes problems disappear. Song makes a heavy heart light.

When there's a song in one's heart, it sustains one through the tests of life.

My little granddaughter always asks, "Grandma, why are you always singing? It's a part of me. I don't even realize I'm doing it. Sometimes I find myself humming in the grocery store.

I believe that everyone can have a song in their heart. Sadness makes the heart heavy and it's hard to be at peace. One feels weighed down with feelings of discouragement and despair.

Anxiety in the heart of a man causes depression. But a good word makes it glad. Proverbs 12:25
A merry heart does good, like medicine, but a broken spirit dries up the bones. Proverbs 17:22

Music has a way of lifting up the spirit and soothing a lonely heart.

Music is a great tool in worship. It can lead one into the presence of God and prepare one to receive from God. Music is important in our worship services to God. In worship we are worshipping God for who he is and giving him the glory and honor due his name. Praise on the other hand is praising God for what he has done for us through his greatness.

Poetry many times is turned into music expressing the heart of the worshipper. God created different forms of expression because different things minister differently to different people. Praise moves some people while worship moves others.

Poem

A Song within my Heart

There is a song within my heart, a song of peace and love.

A song that only the Spirit can give,

It comes from God above.

Sometimes this song comes forth in adoration for the one who placed it there.

Sometimes it comes through a shout of joy.

It's a song of celebration.

Sometimes this song is still and quiet, sometimes it fills the air.

No matter what I'm going through, the song is always there.

As I look to the one who gave the song,

I know the answer always comes.

I don't fear the things that come against me.

I don't fear the things that come my way.

I know the trials are temporal and subject to change.

They are not here to stay.

Nothing can take this song away.

Peace and joy come forth as I begin to sing.

There's been this something special, right from the start.

It's the thing that keeps me going, the song within my heart.

The Place Where I Belong

Many go through life never finding their place. They go from place to place trying to fit in somewhere. They try different relationships hoping to find fulfillment in someone else. They try different jobs and different churches, not realizing the void is in their own heart.

Every human being is born with a void that they try to satisfy with other things. For some it is fame and fortune, for others they might try to fill the void with drugs, yet others try to fill it with sex and relationships.
No matter what we do, we still find ourselves longing for something more. God is the only one who can fill that void so that we don't have to keep searching for something. He is the only one who can satisfy the emptiness we feel inside our soul.

True riches are found in God. So many have gone down the road of fame and fortune only to find that the void in their heart has only increased. They find that there is still something lacking in their life. That something that the world is searching for and we all need cannot be bought. It is a gift that is freely given to us. Everyone is looking for peace in one's heart. True peace only comes from the Prince of peace. Jesus said he has given us his peace. Not the kind of peace the world gives. The world's peace depends on circumstances.

If everything is going our way we are at peace but as soon as things begin to change our peace is gone. Many people seem to enjoy unrest and look for ways to disrupt peace. Even though there may be chaos all around us, we can still have peace in our heart if our peace comes from God and not our circumstances.

God has good plans for you. He created you with a plan and a purpose for your life. Peace is part of that plan. Fulfillment is also a part of that plan. All of it is found in a relationship with Jesus Christ.

> Peace I leave with you, my peace I give to you: not as the world gives do I give to you. Let not your heart be troubled, neither let it be afraid. John 14:27

When the scripture says let not, it means that you can prevent your heart from being troubled and you can keep your heart from being afraid, it's up to you.

I have lived with trouble and unrest and I have been at peace and peace is better. It's wonderful to lie down at night and be able to close my eyes and sleep because my heart is at rest. I know in whom I have believed and I know that he never sleeps and he never leaves me nor forsakes me. While I'm resting he is working. He causes all things to work together for my good according to Romans 8:28.

> And we know that all things work together for good to those who love God, to those who are the called according to His purpose.

Maybe you're thinking yeah, that's for those who are called, the ministers. No, everyone who believes in Jesus Christ is called according to God's purpose. You to, can sleep at night without a worry in your heart. I said before that I used to worry about everything. It kept me awake at night, trying to figure out how I was going to make things work. When I began to get into the word, I began to find out that God wants me to cast my cares upon him because he cares for me. After years of trying to figure out how to make things work I finally came to the conclusion that if I don't have answers I can't make them work, but, I know someone who has the answers and someone who can make things work. I've learned that if I can change things to change them if I can't to let them go.

I see people struggling to change things they cannot change and it's the hardest thing to get them to see how doing that is just wasting their time and frustrating them. Why live with frustration if one doesn't have to. Some think if they don't worry, who is going to do it? Don't we live in a fallen world filled with frustrations? Yes, we live in a fallen world and yes there are frustrations in the world but Jesus said we are in the world but we're not of it. The things that affect the world don't have to affect us.

Jesus came to show us a better way if we follow him, a way of quiet peace and tranquility.

> And ye shall know the truth, and the truth shall make you free.
> John 8:32

The truth of God's word sets us free from the lies of the world and the traditions of men and religion. God seeks relationship not religion. Religion can't save but God can. If you are seeking for the place where you belong, I encourage you to seek the Lord. In him you will find where you belong and you will find your true identity.

Poem

The Place Where I Belong

I've found the place where I belong

The place I've searched for, for so long.

I've come through many tests and trials, traveled many roads for many miles.

And all the time it was right before me

Because of the blindness of my eyes, I could not see

Jesus said the Kingdom of God is within you

How can it be?

I couldn't see how any good thing, could be in me.

He said, it doesn't come by what you see.

It's not something you can buy with gold.

What I have placed within you is free.

You've got to look within and then you'll see.

All this time I've been in thee.

All you'll ever need is found in me.

In this kingdom there is peace.

You can spend the rest of your days at ease.

I just trust in him and he provides as long as in him I abide.

Now within my heart there is a song.

I've found the place where I belong.

Encouragement at a Time of Loss

Every one of us at one time or other has lost a loved one or someone dear. Many times there are questions raised to which there seems to be no answers.

When one is grieving over a loved one, that person often times is so overwhelmed with feelings that he or she tends to forget that others are grieving also.

At that time no one wants to hear someone say "they're in a better place." Or, God needed another angel in heaven. It's true that if someone dies in Christ, that he or she is in a better place. But at the time of loss we want to know if anyone else knows what we're going through, if anyone feels our loss, our feeling of despair, our pain. We feel so alone in our sorrow. Our mind is bombarded by thoughts of what could have been. We want to know if anybody understands.

The bible tells us that Jesus is touched with the feelings of our infirmities. He experienced death for us. He took the sting out of death. God knows what you're going through. He understands your pain. He understands your loss. One day his only son hung on a cross.

God is able to bring comfort to your heart that no one else can give. He is able to give you a peace and a hope. Sometimes you just need to crawl up in his arms and let him hold you; let him reassure you that you can go on, that death as final as it seems, is not the end.

The Bible says that the secret things belong to the Lord but the things that are revealed belong to us. There are some questions that are never going to be answered in this lifetime. We may never understand the why but for Christians there are no goodbyes. With that hope, also comes the courage to go on living and to live for Christ so that one day we can be reunited with our loved one.

I wrote a couple of poems for some folks I knew whose loved one passed away. I know it's a difficult time and many times we ourselves don't know how to act or what to say. At times like that, I find myself at a loss for words. I don't know what to say. How can someone who is grieving understand that you really do know what they are going through? What words are appropriate for such a time as this?

Encouragement at a Time of Loss

No one knows what you're going through unless they've been there too.

They don't understand the pain and grief you feel.

They don't understand that the pain is real.

There is one who has been there, one who understands your loss.

One day his only son hung on a cross.

He is touched with the feeling of your infirmity.

And underneath his wings, you find security.

Trust in the Father, he knows best.

He said, come unto me and I will give you rest.

No one can give you peace, like the father above.

Underneath are the everlasting arms of his love

Crawl up in his arms and nestle there.

You will find a peace as gentle as a dove.

The burden seems lighter, the pain you can bear.

Everything is easier when you know someone cares.

Some Things We Don't Understand

Some things are hard to understand, especially when it comes to the passing of a loved one, especially if the passing was sudden and unexpected.

Many times we question God about the why of things. The Bible tells us in *Deuteronomy* 29:29 that the secret things belong to the Lord. What he reveals to us belongs to us. So there are things that we may never know where it concerns life and death.

One thing we can be assured of is that there are no good byes' for Christians. We will see our loved ones again. In Jesus Christ there is no end.

Times like this should encourage us to live for the Lord so that one day we may be reunited with those we love who have gone on before.

There is a place in the Lord where we can find peace and rest. At times like this we can trust in him and know that he is our shelter from the storms of life, a place of safety. He is our refuge and our fortress. We can go to him and know that we are safe in the shadow of his wings. That we can enter into the secret place and find peace. Not peace like the world gives. The peace the world gives is based on circumstances, what is going on around us. The peace that passes understanding is the kind of peace only God can give. In times of loss this is the only kind of peace that can see us through our time of grief.

It's okay to cry as you experience the loss of your loved one. They are healing tears and part of the healing process. The Bible says in *I Thessalonians 4:13* we don't sorrow as the world does and that is because we know that death is not the end, we will one day be reunited with our loved one again. The world sorrows because they have no hope. They don't have the assurance that their loved one is with the Lord.

Our assurance comes because we believe that Jesus died for our sins and that when we repent and receive him as our Lord and Savior, he forgives us of all of our sins and cleanses us from all unrighteousness according to *I John 1:9*. We then have the assurance that when we die we will go to be with the Lord. He is waiting for us with open arms. The bible also tells us that to be absent from the body is to be present with the Lord. Angels carry your loved one into the arms of Jesus.

Poem

Some things we don't understand

Some things we will never know.

The secret things belong to the Lord.

We may never understand the why.

One thing we can be sure of, the Word is so.

There are no goodbyes for Christians.

In Christ there is no end.

There's a stronger desire to live for him, so that one day we will be united again.

Yes there is grieving and yes there is pain.

We don't sorrow as the world that has no hope.

We know there is sunshine after the rain.

When the pain is overwhelming and you feel like you're weakening in your race, remember, there's always that secret place, where the Lord holds you in his embrace.

The pain and hurts seem to be erased, as you gaze into his loving face

Appreciation

Everyone needs to feel like he or she is appreciated. It's a part of our human nature. We want some sort of response from those we do things for. Not that we're seeking the praises of man, but it's good to know that what we do is appreciated.

Many people have a servant's heart. Serving comes natural to them. For other's it must be a choice they make. A servant is always doing something for others. Many times the things they do seem to go unnoticed in the hustle and bustle of life.

One could be having a bad day and all one needs is a little encouragement to lift ones spirits up. All of us have kind words we can give. Sometimes all it takes is a smile. Speaking kind words to someone and seeing them smile lifts up the spirit of the one speaking the kind words and touches the heart of the one spoken to.

If you are a person with a servant's heart, don't ever stop being a blessing to others. If it seems that no one notices the things you do here on this earth, be assured that God keeps good records and he will reward your good works.

> *And behold, I come quickly; and my reward is with me, to give to every man according as his work shall be. Revelation 22:12*

There's a great need in our world to be more sensitive to the needs of others. It's always nice to receive a compliment for a job well done. God is taking note of our good works and one day pay day will come.

We live in a society today which is very selfish. The bible speaks of a time in history when people will be lovers of self. I have never before seen the self-centeredness on the scale I'm seeing it today. It's all about me. It's all about my needs, my wants. We are unknowingly fulfilling bible prophecy.

Jesus said we are to have love one to another. Love prefers the other person. Love is not self seeking. There is no place for self-centeredness in the heart of a servant. Having a servant's heart is a gift from God. Having a servant's heart is priceless. A servant is always ready to serve another. Our Lord Jesus Christ had a servant's heart. He did not come to earth to be served. He came to serve humanity. Now after his death, burial, and resurrection we serve him. We do it because of the gratitude of our heart for what he has done for us. In like manner we should appreciate the things that others do for us.

Many times we overlook or forget the things others do for us. We fail to show appreciation. Many times that person has gone out of his or her way to do something nice for us. It could have been a sacrifice on their part.

People need to feel appreciated and to know that the things they do for others don't always go unnoticed. Sometimes all a person needs to hear is thank you.

If you are a person with a servant's heart I can assure you that the Lord sees every good deed you do. One day you will receive your reward and your reward will be great.

Poem

In Appreciation

This poem is written in appreciation for all the things you do.

I'm forever grateful for someone like you.

Your kind words and your thoughtful ways always make my day.

Thank you is not enough to express the gratitude of my heart.

I could see there was something special about you right from the start.

God puts a little bit of himself into everything he creates.

Those little things are what make someone like you, great.

Never let go of that servant's heart.

It will take you to greater heights.

It will broaden your horizons and expand your sight.

As you walk in his footsteps, you will always walk in light and everything you do will always turn out right.

Marriage Is a Covenant

This poem came to me when my son and daughter in law were planning their wedding.

Marriage is more than walking down the aisle and saying I do. It's more than a man and a woman making a life together. Marriages are made.

There's no manual that can tell you certain steps to take to make a marriage work. Each case is different. Every individual is different. We all have different temperaments, different likes and dislikes. Marriage is two entirely different individuals trying to work together with two different personalities. It takes hard work to make a successful marriage.

Marriage is not a contract. You can't find any hidden reasons for divorce, no hidden clauses to help you get out of it. Marriage is a covenant between a man and a woman in love. A covenant is much stronger than a contract. A covenant is not only between two people, it's also a covenant between two spirits in the sight of God. Marriage is a holy union instituted by God himself.

A covenant is much more binding than a contract. A covenant says what is mine is yours and what is yours is mine. It's a hundred percent giving one to another.

Today we live in a society where marriage is not looked upon with favor because too many marriages end in divorce. Many people prefer to live together with the privileges of marriage without true responsibility to the other person.

I don't believe that two people who practice the love of God will ever end up in divorce court. The bible says in *1 Corinthians 13:4-8* that love is long suffering and is kind. Love doesn't envy or seek its own. Love doesn't lift up itself. It is not puffed up. It is not easily provoked. It doesn't think evil. It doesn't rejoice in iniquity but rejoices in the truth. Love bears all things, hopes all things, and endures all things. Love never fails.

If all married people practiced what the bible says and walked in the God kind of love, they would never end up in divorce court. They would have consideration for one another instead of being self-centered. Some are longsuffering but not kind. When our mate says something that rubs us the wrong way we don't respond in love, rather we tend to get upset and say things we shouldn't say. Love is not easily provoked. It takes a lot of patience to remain calm when one is provoked. It takes a lot of practice in practicing being slow to speak.

Many marriages suffer because one or the other is a selfish person seeking his or her own satisfaction. Marriage has no place for selfishness.
Some say you have to give fifty, fifty per cent. In reality each has to be willing to give a hundred percent. In every relationship there are the givers and the takers. In order to have a successful marriage one should try to out give the other. One can never out give the other if he or she is a giver. When you give, God keeps giving back to you. Jesus said it is *more blessed to give than to receive.*

They say ministry is spelled w-o-r-k. Marriage is also spelled w-o-r-k. If you don't work at making your marriage a success it will surely fail.

I'm not speaking of marriage from the standpoint of one who has no experience. I have been married to my husband for forty one years now.

I can tell you it takes lots of work. I can also tell you, your marriage can succeed. My marriage has been a success because neither my husband nor I are quitters. Yes we had our bad times. We had our arguments over silly little things that didn't mean anything. We had our ups and downs. Once we got serious about it, we began to work to make it a success.

Right now I can say I am married to the best man in the world. I attribute it to Jesus being the center of our marriage. And we have determined to let the peace of God be the settling factor in all decisions that we make. If we don't have peace about something we are about to do, we won't move until we both have peace in our heart. We have learned to agree on all major decisions. We have come a long way from where we were in the beginning.

There is nothing more beautiful than a husband and wife who are equally yoked in the spirit. We are both in ministry. It's not his ministry and my ministry. It's our ministry. He is behind me a hundred per cent and I do the same for him. We are not competing in ministry. We complement one another.

Marriage is not made in heaven or hell. Marriage is made on earth. Marriage is what you make it.

Poem

Marriage Is

Marriage is a covenant between two hearts in love.

It's a sign of God's approval, a binding from above.

What God has joined together, let no man put asunder.

It's a union of two spirits, one of God's greatest wonders.

Marriage is a life time of growing closer day by day, of knowing one another in an intimate way.

Building the relationship based on God's love, built upon the word of God and direction from above.

It takes two to make a marriage, two hearts becoming one.

It's work that takes a life time, a work that's never done.

A lifetime of giving, a lifetime of sharing, a lifetime of holding and a lifetime of caring.

Marriage holds no secrets, in one another you must confide, trusting one another as you grow side by side.

If you keep God in your marriage, it will keep you from going wrong.

If you keep him in your marriage, it will make your marriage strong.

Your union will be blessed, if it's a union based on love.

And always takes instruction and direction from the father of love.

Two Hearts Knit in Love

I wrote this poem one day as I was thinking about what it takes to make love a success.

It's easy to say I love you. Love is more than just saying I love you. Love is more than mere words. Love is something that grows out of the heart. Love like marriage does not happen automatically. Yes the attraction is there, but love is much more than attraction. One can be attracted to another as a physical attraction without love.

True love is willing to go the limit, whatever it takes. We talked about love in marriage in the previous chapter. Marriage takes two hearts knit in love in order to survive.

We live in a day when anything goes and we have to safeguard our marriages.

Marriage is still sacred in the eyes of God. God smiles down on marriages that succeed. Success comes through much patience and hard work. If your goal is to make a go of your marriage you have to work extra hard at it. You have to look at it as a goal you can attain. You can't let other things people are doing cause you to stumble. You have to stay focused. There is no mountain too high that you can't get over. There is no ocean too deep that you cannot get across if your heart is knit in love. Tough times and trying times cannot take your focus off of the Lord. Keeping the Lord in your marriage is the secret ingredient to a successful marriage, as is walking in love.

There's nothing too hard for those who have a genuine relationship based on love. If you have faith that your marriage will succeed, it will.

Poem

Two Hearts Knit

in love

Two hearts in love forever, growing stronger day by day, following God's Spirit, as he leads the way, through mountains high and valleys low, through harsh and barren lands, many times those roads lead through hot and burning sands.

If you keep your eyes focused and your eyes are stayed on him, no matter what the circumstances, you know you will always win.

There's no mountain too high, no river too wide, there's nothing that can stop God's plan, hinder or even hide.

Nothing is impossible when there's a vision given from above and those two hearts continue to be knit in love.

Love Is

Love suffers long and is kind; love does not envy; love does not parade itself, is not puffed up; does not behave rudely, does not seek its own, is not provoked, thinks no evil; does not rejoice in iniquity, but rejoices in the truth; bears all things, believes all things, hopes all things, endures all things. I Corinthians 13:4-7

As long as we follow God's definition of love, love never fails. What does it mean to suffer long? Does it mean we accept everything and anything that comes in the name of love? No! It means that love grows to the place where it is able to tolerate some things, to make compromises and adjustments without getting upset.

If couples walked in the God kind of love there would be no room for divorce. Divorce comes from selfishness and intolerance, and rising to the occasion when provoked.

I've been married to my husband for forty one years. It wasn't always a bed of roses. We had our differences that caused many fights and arguments. We missed out on love's blessings because we couldn't understand our differences.

It's easy to fall in love. It's harder to stay in love once you really get to know the person you married. Now you see not only the good side of the person you married but the bad side also. We tend to let our hair down. We're not trying to impress anymore. We had to learn to make adjustments along the way. Marriage is a lifetime of adjusting to one another. It's a lifetime of giving. We have to allow the other person to be his or her self and to be able to express his or her opinion without feeling intimidated by the other person.

Poem

Love Is

Love is sharing the important things in life with someone who really cares.

Love is sharing your innermost thoughts and dreams.

You are never left alone to face life on your own.

Love is, understanding one another, when the going gets tough.

Life has its ups and downs and sometimes the road gets rough.

When God is the center of everything you do, life is so much easier because his grace rests upon you.

No matter what comes your way, he will always see you through.

The Meaning of Love

What does love mean? Does anybody know what real love is? Young people think they are in love when they meet the person of their dreams but cam that person really love the other person without knowing that one? I heard one woman say she thought she was in love when she first met her husband to be but found out that it was only puppy love. Real love came after years of living with that person and adjusting to him. I can attest to that after being married forty one years to the same man. I thought I loved him when we first met but I didn't know him like I do now. I didn't know the adjustments I would have to make along the way and the things only love can put up with at times. I didn't know the tests and trials of life we would face together and the trying times that only true love can endure.

Many young people make the mistake of thinking they are in love when in fact it is only puppy love. Many mistakes are made in the name of love by young and old alike. Older people many times make mistakes because many refuse to grow up and face reality.

Thank God that there are still many who have made a go of their marriages even when some have thought they might have made a mistake in the beginning. Many times the bigger mistake is not working out our differences and learning to overlook the little things that are unimportant.

I've seen many marriages end in divorce because the couple was unwilling to work things out. Many times those people end up in similar situations over and over again because they haven't learned to overcome the real issue.

Poem

The Meaning of Love

Love is sharing your life with another, sharing your innermost thoughts, knowing there is someone who understands you, someone who really cares.

Real love is sharing your faith with another of like precious faith, strengthening and encouraging one another to go on in the things that really matter.

Love is fulfilling the plan of God for your life and running your race with patience.

Love is keeping God in your relationship as your leader and guide, keeping everything in the open with nothing to hide.

Love is living every day with wisdom and love.

Love seeks direction for everything that comes from our Father up above.

On Your Special Day

This poem was written for my granddaughter's wedding on March 17th of 2011. It was a cool day with a little breeze. The wedding was held outside at the Atrium at Grandville Arts Center in Garland Texas. The trees hadn't put out their leaves yet so they were kind of bare but nobody's thoughts or focus were on the trees that day, everyone's attention was centered on the beautiful bride walking down the aisle on her father's arm.

The preacher and the groom were waiting with great expectancy as they watched this beautiful young woman walk down the aisle. This was a special occasion for both granddaughter and grandfather when Dominique's grandfather would have the privilege of joining Dominique and Adrian together in Holy Matrimony.

A wedding is always a special occasion but it's even more special when the bride is your daughter or granddaughter. In this case, on this special occasion it was our granddaughter's wedding. It was even more special to her because her grandfather got to perform the ceremony and that made it extra special. For him it was something he had dreamed about and looked forward to doing for some time.

We were privileged to watch this young lady as she was growing up. Her mother was in a car accident when Dominique was two years old. That car accident left her mother in a wheel chair with limited abilities. Dominique grew up with her father because her mother was unable to care for her so we were privileged to have her and her brother on holidays and during the summer when school was out.

Dominique is about four feet ten inches tall. She is a very petite young lady. When she was little she would say, "I'm getting bigger, right grandpa." As you can see she didn't grow much bigger.

Dominique and Adrian knew each other since junior high. They both attended Garland Jr. High and high school together and much of their college days. She was looking forward to the day he would propose to her.

At the time of this writing she is preparing to teach in Memphis Tennessee this fall. I desire nothing but the best for her and Adrian. I believe their love has been proven through the years and together they can face the world.

Poem

On Your Special Day

We gather here today in the presence of the Lord, to join two hearts in love with God's blessing from above.

Marriage is not a contract and it's not an act.

Marriage is a covenant that keeps your love intact.

A covenant is not a ceremony but a joining of two spirits and making them one.

It's not just going through the motions and it's done. It takes a lifetime of becoming one.

It takes working out your differences with love and concern, giving of yourself is a lesson you will learn.

It's not 50, 50 as some would say, it's giving 100% every day.

Love is not self-seeking, love is kind.

Love is quick to forgive and leave the hurts behind.

Love is always moving forward gaining momentum day by day, learning to love one another every step of the way.

Love bears up under everything and anything that comes.

Love will always and under every circumstance, overcome.

Two hearts joined together by the Father up above will forever be for you a token of your love.

When times get rough and things seem hard because of the days, remember God is with you each step of the way and the commitment you make today will guide you on your way.

Thinking of you

Have you ever stopped to think about your relationship with the one you love? I sometimes think about the time when my husband and I first met. I often think about how our relationship got started, and where we are now.

It didn't start out where we're at now. It would have saved a lot of heart ache and tears. We started out in a humble little home, we didn't have much but we had each other. Many times we wanted to quit because the going got tough but something in us kept us going.

We did without a lot of things but we never lacked in love. Yes there have been times when we wished we had never met. It wasn't always easy. We had a lot of adjusting to do.

Our relationship throughout the years has become precious and dear.
I thank the Lord because if it had not been for him, we wouldn't be where we are today.

Today we enjoy the goodness of the Lord. Our love has grown over the years. It seems like our hearts can't grow much fonder. Every year we are drawn closer together. We have weathered the storms that rose up against us. We have faced the giants of lack and fear and come out victorious. We have walked through the shadow of death but every time his rod and staff comforted us.

There is nothing that can compare to the security one feels when one has confidence in the person he or she loves. I thank God for the man my husband has turned out to be and I give God all the credit for fashioning him and making him into the man he is today.

There was a time I didn't know what was going to become of our marriage. We struggled with many things and fought over everything. Many times we felt like our marriage was on a downward spin. We held on to one another. Later we came to know the Lord and our downward spin began to reverse itself and make an upward climb.

I write about many things but writing about marriage is always a blessing to me because we have succeeded in our marriage.

I wrote this poem while thinking of where we began our journey together to where we are now.

Poem

Thinking of You

Today I've been thinking of you, the friendship we share and the things we do.

I'm thinking about the things we do together and how when we're together time seems to fly.

I think about the good times and the bad, the times we laugh and the times we cry.

I thank God for that special binding of two hearts in love, sealed forever by God above.

I'm thinking about the joy and the things we share. There's nothing in the world that can ever compare, to the security I feel just in knowing you care.

Knowing you will always be there by my side.

There will never be anything between us that we have to hide.

Together we can soar on eagles wings, as the wind and the breeze softly sing.

We're flying far and high above, gentle as a dove, to greater and greater heights on the wings of love.

The Change I see in you

Therefore if any man be in Christ, he is a new creature: old things are passed away, behold, all things are become new.
2 Corinthians 5:17

I have been in ministry long enough to see the change that takes place when a person accepts Christ and begins to walk in the word.

The change takes place on the inside first and then begins to manifest itself on the outside.

I wrote this poem for a young lady graduating from high school. She was a very shy person, very introverted. She was the type of person that bullies love to bully. All through school she felt intimidated by other classmates. She had a love for animals and always desired to work with them. The other kids thought she was strange because she wasn't out doing what other teenagers were doing

During her last year of high school her parents sent her to a Christian school to see if that would help her come out of her shell.

This young lady went from a shy, intimidated person to a very sweet and likable person. There was such an incredible change that took place, you couldn't help but take note of it.

I wrote this poem on her graduation in honor of the transformation I could see in her.

There is an obvious transformation that takes place when one comes to know who one is in Christ. One no longer has to identify with what the world wants one to identify with. It takes time in the word of God to grow. We were programmed in the ways of the world before we came to the Lord. After receiving him we have to change direction and begin to reprogram ourselves to his ways. It's easier to go with the flow than to go against the current. Many people don't want to change because they would rather take the path of least resistance. It takes work and many people don't want to work.

It also takes much patience that's why many people get discouraged and quit.

Seeing ourselves in the word of God helps us identify with the way God sees us. The word of God is like a mirror. It not only shows us our imperfections but it also shows us our good points. We can take those good points and work on them to make us better. We can take what we don't like and improve our attitudes.

I marvel at what God can do. I marvel at how he can take a person who is shy and intimidated and turn that person into a beautiful person. It's like watching a butterfly struggling to come out of that ugly cocoon, day after day working its way out. One day when you least expect it a butterfly emerges. The work is over, now it can spread its wings and fly. It's wonderful to see the transformation that takes place with love from God above. It takes a person to new heights and new levels. It assures one of the fathers love.

Poem

The Change I see in You

It's all so incredible, the change that's come over you.

I always stand amazed at the things that God can do.

All it took was a little love from God above, to transform your life and make you as gentle as a dove.

Encouragement alone does so many wonderful things.

It causes you to rise up with power in your wings.

Even though in times past, you might have suffered pain, God took your life and transformed it like a flower after the rain.

Like the sun which has been shinning on the petals for awhile, he has given you godly character and a winning smile.

Those characteristics will take you further than you know. If you allow the Holy Spirit to guide you as you go. He's molding you and making you into what you need to be.

One day when he's finished the whole world will see.

It was the love of God that made you so free.

Now you can soar to new heights and levels.

Nothing can stop you, not even devils.

Keep your faith and trust in God, as you continue to move in the power of his love.

What Gift Could I Bring

As Christmas was approaching one day I found myself thinking, if I could go before the Lord what gift could I bring that would be sufficient for all he's done for me?

Is there anything worthy to bring before him? Can I buy a gift that can make up for the pain and suffering he endured in my place? There is no price that we can pay in order to repay a debt that has been paid for us. No amount of money, no amount of gold or silver is sufficient to pay the debt we owed.
We were lost and without God. We had no direction. We were just following the course of this world. We were living in sin unaware of sin's consequences.

> For the wages of sin is death; but the gift of God is eternal life
> through Jesus Christ our Lord. Romans 6:23

Thank God that even while we were yet sinners according to Romans 5:8, Christ died for us.

Christmas these days is not what it used to be.
I remember growing up singing Christmas carols about the Lord. Our

school programs consisted of angels and wise men and Mary and Joseph and the baby Jesus in a manger. We sang songs like Away in a manger, Silent Night, O little Town of Bethlehem in school and no one complained no one was offended. Now one can't put a nativity scene on one's own property if it offends someone. Our children can't even sing in school about Jesus. In fact they know more about Santa than they do about Jesus. Christmas is so commercialized that children grow up thinking it's all about Santa and gifts. Santa is just a figment of someone's imagination. He has never done anything for anyone except lead them astray through deception.

When our granddaughter was small we told her Santa wasn't real. She looked at us as if to say "where have you been?" She knew Santa was real, she had seen him at the mall. It's hard to tell children about Jesus when they have been taught to believe a lie.

People don't want anyone to offend them but they think nothing of offending God every day with the things they do and say.

We all have a choice where offenses are concerned. We can choose to overlook an offense or we can choose to allow things we don't agree with to become a stumbling block in our life. Not only do they become a stumbling block but a stronghold that in time controls our very actions. Offenses are guaranteed to come. There is no way around them, there's no way over them. Jesus said they would come. It takes humility to overlook an offense, not allowing it to take control of our actions. Most of the time the person who offended us, isn't even aware that we have been offended. Many times the person offended doesn't even realize they are being controlled by the person who offended them.

There is no way we can ever repay the Lord for what he's done for us. The best gift any of us can bring before the Lord is a humble heart.
God doesn't ask for much in return. He only looks for hearts that are surrendered to him. He gave it all for us. What can we give to him?

Poem

What Gift Could I Bring?

Thinking of the wise men and the gifts they brought that day,

I wondered what gift I could bring that was fit for a King.

I had nothing to offer him, I had nothing to bring.

I knelt down beside him, humbled and broken, heavy with my sin.

I said, Lord I have nothing to bring before my King. My emptiness and broken heart is hardly a gift to bring.

He said "my child, that gift is all that is required to come before the King."

"It's not the price you pay that determines your worth; it's the price I paid so that you could have new birth."

"Your heart is a priceless thing to bring before the King.

I can take it and mold it and make it a beautiful thing."

Then I heard the voices of a thousand angels sing.

The Lord said, they are rejoicing over the gift you bring.

A humble heart and a contrite spirit is a very costly thing.

It's the best gift one can bring before the King of Kings.

The Cost of Christmas

Christmas is a beautiful time of year. It's the time that Christians everywhere celebrate the birth of our Lord. It's true that we don't know the exact date of his birth but we know he was born and we know why he came to earth. To argue over the date is fruitless. It's not the date that's important it's what his birth represents that is important.

The meaning of Christmas has been lost in all the hustle and bustle of the season. Many people don't even know Jesus was born with a purpose and that the purpose was to live and die so we could have new birth. They get caught up in the world's view of Christmas and are distracted by all the glamour the season presents. It's just as it happened when Jesus was born. People were going about their business unaware that the greatest event in history was about to take place in a humble manger. They were caught up in the cares of the day.

Jesus wasn't born in a hospital or a fancy hotel. There wasn't room found at the inn for Mary and Joseph and the soon coming King. They had to make due with a stable, Jesus humble beginning.

People were unaware of the price this child would pay one day. They didn't have a clue that he would one day die for me and you. People are still busy doing their own thing. They are unaware of the meaning of the season. With all the running to and fro, they get caught up in the hustle and bustle and forget that Christmas is more than buying and spending. It's much more than giving and receiving gifts. Much more than spending money they don't have to spend. Minds are no longer on the meaning of Christmas but on the gifts one receives.

Christmas comes and goes each year and we get further and further away from the true meaning of the season we celebrate. We celebrate Christmas because we recall the event of our Savior's birth and how God so loved the world according to John 3:16, that he gave his only begotten son, so that whosoever believes in him should not perish but have everlasting life.

If Jesus had not come into this world as a baby, none of us would have a chance. He came in human form in order that he might know what it's like to live in a sinful world and overcome sin. Taking on human form made him able to relate to our pain and suffering. It's good to know that we have a Savior that is able to relate to us and the things we go through. He was willing to lay down his life for us so that we could be forgiven and given new life.

I wrote this poem while in Georgia in the year 2000.

Poem

The Cost of Christmas

We've gotten so far from the real thing, the meaning we have lost.

Before Jesus came into this world he had already considered the cost, the cost to reconcile a lost world gone astray, the price of Calvary, the cost he'd have to pay.

He suffered agony in the Garden and separation from the Father, the shame, the torment and dying for another.

Not for a righteous man but one lost in sin, a destiny foretold, a lost and dying world to win.

It all began with an innocent baby laid in a bed of hay.

Not a royal palace or even a fancy inn, not even a hotel was available that day.

Everyone was busy going their own way, unaware that anything special had taken place that day, unaware of who this baby boy was sleeping in the hay.

They were unaware of the pain and suffering he would have to face; unaware that anything was wrong with the human race.

Two thousand years have come and gone, another Christmas is here.

People are still busy doing their own thing, still unaware of the meaning of Christmas and significance of the year.

It's the dawning of a new age, the passing of the old, of things that are coming, things which have been foretold.

Jesus is the reason for the season from the start.

The meaning of Christmas begins by receiving him in one's heart.

If the real meaning of Christmas we hold dear and know in one's heart his return is near, if we know his word, if we believe his promise, the real meaning of Christmas will never be far from us.

The end of two thousand years marks a significant phase.

The coming years will be years to embrace.

The prophets of old spoke of these days.

As we pick up the pace and stay in this race, as we continue to seek him and walk in his ways, we will remain steadfast in these last days and soon we will see him face to face.

Nowhere to Turn

There are many people in this world who have come to the end of their rope and it seems there is nowhere to turn, nowhere to run, no one that cares.

You can run but you can't hide from yourself. Everywhere you go you are there. Everywhere you turn you are there and you can't get away from yourself, so you keep on running but getting nowhere.

Many people reach the place where nothing really matters anymore. They are tired of their lifestyle but don't know who to turn to for help. So they reach the conclusion that there is no one to help them escape the bondage they are living in. Their life takes one bad turn after another that isn't getting them anywhere. Their mind is filled with thoughts of failure and regret for things they cannot change.

At the writing of this book an acquaintance of my daughter's committed suicide by hanging himself. He was in and out of rehab centers and I'm sure he was discouraged with life. He probably felt like there was no hope left.

If you find yourself in this condition, there is hope. There is someone who can help you turn your life around. The Lord is able to help you turn your life around. You cannot do it on your own.

I personally know people in your condition who have found their help in the Lord. You can't run from yourself and you can't change yourself. One thing you can do is forgive yourself. That's the thing people find the hardest to do. You have lived with yourself, you know yourself better than anyone else. You know your own failures and short comings. At times like these that's all you see.

You've known the Lord, he has never left you. You got away from him. He's still knocking at the door of your heart but you can't hear him because your own pain is too great. When you think of him he seems so far away.

Since I began my walk with the Lord thirty two years ago, I have never gotten away from him but I have been in situations where I felt like God had left me. I couldn't sense his presence. I felt orphaned and alone. If I hadn't known the Lord and known that he has promised in his word to never leave us nor forsake us, I don't know what I would have done. See, I wasn't away from God. I was going to Kingsway Missionary School to learn Spanish. It was a difficult time for me. Spanish was a hard language to learn. I didn't know the area nor did I like it. We lived in cramped quarters with limited income. It seemed like I ate verbs, I dreamed verbs, I spoke verbs, and I wrote verbs all day long. I couldn't see God in it. I didn't seem to have the time I had with the Lord and felt spiritually dry.

Now as I look back I can see how difficult it would be now if I had not learned the language. It has been a blessing as I am now involved in teaching in a Spanish speaking church. That has been the only time I felt like God was far away or at the least hiding himself from me. Sometimes I think he does that to test our faithfulness.

I personally know a person who was addicted to drugs; this poem was written for him. I saw his struggle with himself. I saw the pain and torment he put himself through. It hurt to see him struggling with himself and myself feeling so helpless to do anything about it.

I know where drugs can take you. They take you further than you want to go and keep you longer than you want to stay. They entrap you so that you find yourself cornered. It didn't start out that way, it never does. At first it made you feel invincible, like nothing was impossible. You felt great but you couldn't stay there without paying a price. Sin always has a price.

> For the wages of sin is death, but the gift of God is eternal life in
> Christ Jesus our Lord. Romans 6:23

The wages of sin is death. Sin will always take you down the road that leads to death. God offers you a free gift. All you have to do is receive it

Drugs have a way of clouding your thinking processes. It's not only drugs that cloud your thinking. There are many other things that take your mind away from the Lord.

Many times we have to come face to face with ourselves and admit we have a problem. It's a hard thing to do because we would rather like to think everyone else has a problem. We can handle our problems, we think.

God is always waiting with outstretched arms. There's no place we can go to hide from him. He knows our every move. Best of all he knows our heart. He is still waiting. Are you ready to surrender?

Poem

Nowhere to Turn

God, I thought I had lost it. I didn't know which way to turn.

Nothing really mattered, I felt so lost within.

I had thoughts of loss and failures and things I could not change, things I held against myself, the "me" I couldn't forgive.

Had taken away from me the desire to live.

I was so tired of running, trying to get away from me.

My eyes had been blinded so that I could not see.

When I finally came to the end of my rope, there you were standing offering me hope.

I thought I had lost you, you seemed so far away.

There you were beside me waiting for me to see, your hand of mercy reaching out to me.

I had to stop running in order to be set free.

So here I am surrendered, Lord, I give myself to thee.

I found I can't get away from you, no matter where I flee.

So here I am Lord forgive me, no more running away from thee.

For you have made me see, the only life worth living is the life I live for thee.

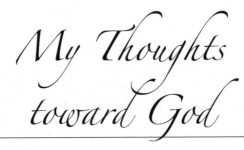

My Thoughts toward God

Thou wilt keep him in perfect peace whose mind is stayed on thee: because he trusteth in thee. Isaiah 26:3

The Bible tells us that we will have perfect peace if we keep our minds on him and trust him. It's so easy to get our minds off of the Lord, especially in the days we are living in. There is so much going on that we had never seen before. There are so many things that distract us and occupy our thoughts daily.

I find peace when I'm in my home in Branson Missouri because my TV is not connected to a cable or dish. I don't see the evening news, so I don't know what's happening in the world. There is peace and tranquility all around me which is why I like to come here to write. Branson has an atmosphere of peace. I can sense it every time I come here.

The Bible tells us what God's thoughts are toward us. Jeremiah 29:11 tells us in the amplified bible: *For I know the thoughts that I think toward you, saith the Lord, thoughts of peace and not of evil, to give you an expected end.*

God's thoughts toward us are good thoughts. They are of peace and not of evil. God wants to give us an expected end, something to hang on to, something to look forward to, something to propel us forward.

When we know how much God loves us, it is easy to keep our minds on Him.

If you don't know what the bible has to say about the end times or the times we are living in, the things you see and hear today can cause fear to enter into your heart. We have nothing to fear when we know we are secure in him.

I like to meditate on the greatness of my God. I stand in awe of him when I contemplate the length he went to, to rescue my soul. I like to think that if I was the only person on the face of the earth he would still have died for me.

> For this reason I bow my knees to the father of our Lord Jesus Christ, from whom the whole family in heaven and earth is named, that he would grant you, according to the riches of his glory, to be strengthened with might through His Spirit in the inner man, that Christ may dwell in your hearts through faith; that you being rooted and grounded in love, may comprehend with all the saints what is the width and length and depth and height—to know the love of Christ which passes knowledge; that you may be filled with the fullness of God.
> Ephesians 3:14-19

God demonstrated his love for us through Jesus. In doing so we were put back in right standing with God. Sin had separated us from God. We can now come before God with boldness, unashamed and without fear.

> Let us therefore come boldly to the throne room of grace that we may obtain mercy and find grace to help in time of need.
> Hebrews 4:16

The scripture before this is talking about how we now have a great High Priest who has passed through the heavens, Jesus the son of God. He has gone before us as our high priest with his own blood to purchase our redemption. It's all because of his blood that we now have access into the presence of God.

Poem

My thoughts Toward God

Lord I stand in awe of you and the love you've shown me.

Sometimes I feel your presence and your glory all around me.

I always picture myself on my face before you, hugging your feet. I guess to me they're precious because they walked to Calvary and you didn't protest when the nails were driven through for me.

The nails represent my sin, nailed to the tree, giving me the opportunity to be set free.

Though I was a sinner and I didn't deserve to live, it was for that purpose that your life you came to give.

I never want to grow cold or tire of what I do for you, whatever your plan for my life is, that's what I want to do.

I want to daily worship at your throne and express my love for you.

I love you Jesus, my Lord and Master you will always be.

All the treasures and wisdom of God are hid in thee.

You're my Lord and King you mean so much to me.

I want my life to revolve around you so all the world can see a little bit of you radiating out of me.

A River Of Blood

And according to the law almost all things are purified with blood, and without the shedding of blood there is no remission. Hebrews 9:22

It was necessary for Jesus to have shed his blood for the remission of sin.

It was the only thing that could purchase the redemption of mankind. Adam and Eve's sin in the Garden of Eden brought a separation between God and man. God is holy. The only way that separation could be gapped was by the blood of a righteous man. We know that there were no righteous men on the earth. The bible says all have sinned and come short of the glory of God. Mankind needed a redeemer, so God sent his only begotten Son into the world in the form and likeness of man. Jesus took our place in his death. It was our debt not his. But being unrighteous in ourselves there was no way we could pay the debt. God needed a sinless sacrifice, a living sacrifice.

Hebrews 10:5-7 therefore when he came into the world, he said, Sacrifice and offering you did not desire, but a body you have prepared for me. In burnt offerings and sacrifices for sin you had no pleasure. Then I said, Behold, I have come, In the volume of the book it is written of me, to do your will O God.

The high priest entered into the Holy of Holies once a year and offered burnt offerings and sacrifices for the sins of the people, but those sacrifices could not erase the sin of the people. They could only cover for a year and it had to be done over and over again. It only took one sacrifice of the spotless Lamb of God to cleanse our conscience from dead works, one sacrifice to cleanse our sins forever.

When Jesus rose from the dead he ascended into heaven to offer his blood for our sins. That blood purchased our redemption forever. There is no further need for burnt offerings and sacrifices for sin. There was one final sacrifice, the blood of Jesus. That blood took care of the debt of mankind.

As I sit here writing, we are approaching the Easter season or the day that Christians remember the resurrection of our Lord and Savior Jesus Christ.

I can't help but think of how far away we have gotten from the real meaning of Resurrection Sunday. The world is rushing to and fro unaware of what took place two thousand years ago.

Easter now has taken on a whole different meaning. Now it's all about Easter eggs and the Easter bunny. I have no idea where or when this started. I can't make the connection between the rabbit and the egg and what it has to do with the resurrection of our Lord. When children are asked about the meaning of Easter their first response is "hunting Easter eggs." Children believe what they are taught. I can't help but think that the reason many children don't believe in Jesus is because we have taught them to believe in Santa Clause and we have taught them to believe in the Easter bunny and we teach them to celebrate Halloween, then we want them to believe in Jesus. Two out of the three don't exist so how can they believe in a Jesus they can't see?

When we believe in Jesus we have to believe in faith. Common sense tells us there has to be a higher power than ourselves. If there's not we're in trouble because we have made a mess out of everything and we in our wisdom don't know how to straighten it out. Thank God that we have the word of God to guide us and when we live according to the word and receive the benefits of it, we know the word is truth. We have the evidence of a changed life.

> *2 Corinthians 4:7 But we have this treasure in earthen vessels, that the excellence of the power may be of God and not of us.*

Thank God for the blood, Jesus said it was shed for the forgiveness of sin. The bible says in *Hebrews 12:24* that Jesus is the mediator of the new covenant and his blood speaks better things than that of Abel. Abel was the son of Adam and Eve who was slain by his brother. The blood of Abel cries out for revenge. The blood of Jesus cries out for forgiveness.

Poem

A River of Blood

A river of blood flowed down from the cross on Calvary.

It flowed to pave the way for you and me.

It opens blind eyes and makes them see.

It brings man down upon his knees, that they might see his majesty.

A river flowed from the cross that day, in order to open up a new and living way.

Today my life has been transformed.

By the power of his blood I have been reborn.

Amazing grace poured down for me.

I once was blind but now I see the significance of Calvary.

That's where Jesus paid the price for me.

I see the splendor of his majesty.

I see his hand of mercy extended to you and me.

It's an unending love, full of grace being poured out on the human race.

Wounded and Bleeding

Have you ever meditated on what took place the day Jesus died? What was on his mind as he gave his last breath?

> Therefore we also, since we are surrounded by so great a cloud of witnesses, let us lay aside every weight and sin which so easily ensnares us, and let us run with endurance the race that is set before us, looking unto Jesus, the author and finisher of our faith, who for the joy that was set before him endured the cross, despising the shame, and has sat down at the right hand of the throne of God. Hebrews 12:1-2

The bible tells us that for the joy that was set before him, he endured the cross. Everything Jesus did he did it for you and for me. When he was on that cross, he looked ahead in time and saw you and I lost in our sin in need of a Savior.

He came to this earth with a purpose and a plan. He came in human form so that he could relate to you and I. He lived a sinless life in order to save us from our sin. He was not going to let anything interrupt the plan and purpose of God. Religious people tried to stop him, the devil tried to stop him, but nothing was going to deter him from his purpose.

We were slaves to sin, there was no way we could pay the debt on our own, no way possible to approach God without a mediator. We were prisoners with no way to escape; sin had built prison walls around us.

When Jesus finished the work God gave him to do, the prison doors were opened. Now it's up to you and me. Are we going to walk out those prison doors a free person or are we going to remain inside even though a way of escape has been made? The choice is up to you, the choice is up to me, what will it be?

Poem

Wounded and Bleeding

Wounded and bleeding, Jesus hung on that tree.

Every gasping breath he took, he was thinking of you and me.

Looking far into the future as only he can see, he saw how one day I would receive him and be forever free.

He called me out of darkness and saved me from the enemy.

My redemption's forever sealed throughout eternity.

How amazing is his love for me, how mighty is his grace!

He came to earth to die and save the human race.

It was our sin he bore upon the tree of Calvary.

He died to free us from sin's slavery.

Now I can lift my hands in praise because my chains are gone.

I can fall prostrate on my face and worship God's only Son, as I hear Jesus final words, it is done.

He Is

When you pass through the waters, I will be with you; And through the rivers, they will not overflow you. When you walk through the fire, you shall not be burned, nor shall the flame scorch you. Isaiah 43:2

There has been a debate going on as to who God is or what he is, since the beginning of time. He is different things to different people. The God of the bible is the God I believe in and he has been different things to me at different times. When I am going through tests and trials he is the fourth man in the fire. He is the one who walks through the fire with me so that when it's all said and done I can come out of it victorious and not get burned. Many people go through tests and trials and come out worse off than when the trials began. It's because they forget that God will walk with them through the fires.

The bible says when you walk through the fire you shall not be burned neither shall the flame scorch you or kindle upon you. How many people do you know who have come out of the fire scorched? It seems like the same tests and trials come to the same people over and over again. I believe it's because they have not learned to allow the Lord to walk with them through the storms of life.

When you're going to school, there are tests you have to take and when you fail one of them, you have to take it over again. It seems like many Christians are failing the tests of life and then they wonder why they keep going through the same thing over and over again. We have to be determined that the tests and trials of life are not going to get us down, that we are going to pass every test because we know who is walking with us.

I always go back to the children of Israel and how they wondered in the wilderness for forty years because they didn't learn their lesson. They murmured and complained about everything. They were so dissatisfied with where they were. God gave them opportunities time and time again to pass the test. They knew the power of God. They saw the miracles God did in the land of Egypt. They had seen God open up the Red Sea so that they could cross over on dry ground. The waters didn't overtake them because God was with them. They saw how God took care of them by providing for them in the wilderness and how he was a cloud by day and a fire by night to keep them cool by day and warm by night. They weren't strangers to the power of God. He took them out of the bondage with a strong arm. They soon forgot the things he did for them. Then every time they got themselves into a mess they would cry out to God and he would save them. He finally had to leave them to their own ways and their own ways destroyed them.

God has been faithful in all of his ways. He has been faithful to hear me when I pray, faithful to answer my prayers. He has been true to his word.

I can depend on him to give me a word in season. I have found that he definitely looks after his word to perform it.

God has been a refuge in the storms I've gone through. He has been my shelter from the storms of life. I can run to him and hide and he becomes my hiding place, my safe dwelling place.

Time and again he has been there for me. He promised never to leave me nor forsake me. Even at times when I feel alone I know he is there.

I have crawled up in his lap when I've been sad and I have felt his loving arms around me. He has comforted me when no one else can.

If you put your trust in him he will always come through for you. If you have strayed from him, the way back has not been blocked. He still waits with open arms. When you return home to him, he doesn't accuse you of what you have done. He acts like you had never left just like the father of the prodigal son did. His son had been given the inheritance and left to do his own thing. When he had wasted his inheritance he found himself hungry and feeding swine. In that place he began to think about his father's house and how he never lacked anything. All the time he was gone the father was waiting for him to come home. When the father saw his son coming from a ways off, he ran to him and hugged his neck and kissed him. He didn't scold him. He didn't ask why he had wasted the inheritance. He was just happy that his son who was as good as dead had come home.

God is waiting for you to come home. He is not holding your sins against you. Jesus has paid the price for you. Will you accept him?
God said I Am. God is everything you need him to be.

Poem

He Is

When the storms of life are moving in, I always find my peace within.

When sinking sand is all around, I take my stand on solid ground.

I can sing Amazing grace how sweet the sound.

My victory in him can always be found.

When the trials of life are causing much distress, I run onto Jesus, my strong fortress.

When I walk through the water he is always there.

He helps me with the load I bear.

When I walk through the fires I won't be burned, nor will the flame kindle upon me,

When the fire gets hot and the water is deep, the way out he makes me to see.

God is more powerful than you think.

He will never let you sink.

When you're seeking refuge and to him you turn, he will never let you burn.

Trust in him he will see you through.

He will help you out in everything you do.

If you trust him you will never miss because God is.

My Heart's Desire

I met the Lord in 1979 in a little county Baptist church. When I accepted the Lord as my Lord and Savior he became my heart's desire. I was so hungry to know more about him, I couldn't get enough of the word. I spent hours devouring the word, reading every book I could get my hands on that would help me know this Jesus. Everywhere Jesus was mentioned I was there, I had spent so many years without him now I wanted to know him more and more.

I knew about him, I heard people talk about him, but no one had ever told me I could have a personal relationship with him. It's sad that even today many have never heard that Jesus died for their sin or that they can be forgiven and begin a new life in him.

When I found him I found life. Before I met him I only existed. He has taught me through his word and the help of the Holy Spirit how to live a life that is pleasing to him.

Thank God for ministers who teach what the bible says. There was one particular minister at the time I got born again who helped me build a firm foundation on the word of God. He never let up, he kept saying, put God first place in your life, Let the word of God be final authority in your life. I began to listen to him and to grow in the word. As I grew in the word, as I grew in understanding, I began to do what the word said. Now I can say my feet are planted on solid ground.

One thing I am seeing less and less of is a hunger for the things of God. When I got born again in 1979 people were hungry for God and hungry for the things of God. I remember going to prayer meetings and bible studies, how people were running hard after him. Today there are many churches where there is no move of God because people do not seek after him.

I'm speaking from my experience as a minister and what I am seeing today. At times I wonder, what can one preach to a people who have no desire to go further and have no vision?

We're living in the end times where it has been prophesied that the love of many will grow cold and that people will have itching ears and many will turn to false doctrines and teachings and turn away from the faith. It has also been prophesied by the prophet Isaiah that when darkness covers the earth and gross darkness the people, God's light will rise upon his people and his glory will be seen upon us. That is what I'm waiting for. I'm praying for God's people to arise out of slumber and get hungry for God. In other words I am praying for a move of God the likes of what the world has never seen.

We must be the light. People are perishing every day. If we're not on fire for God we have nothing to attract a lost and dying world to. In the natural when someone sees a fire the first thing they want to do is find out where it's at so they can watch it burn. If we are full of light and God's glory is seen upon us, others are going to be attracted to the light of his glory.

The apostle Paul was a man who loved the Lord. He wrote 2/3 of the New Testament and yet he wanted to know God more and more. He wasn't satisfied with where he was. The apostle Paul sums up his desire which is also my desire, in this way:

Yet indeed I also count all things loss for the excellence of the knowledge of Christ Jesus my Lord for whom I have suffered the loss of all things, and count them as rubbish that I may gain Christ and be found in him, not having my own righteousness, which is from the law, but that which is through faith in Christ, the righteousness which is from God by faith; that I may know him and the power of His resurrection, and the fellowship of His sufferings being conformed to His death, if by any means, I may attain to the resurrection of the dead. Philippians 3:8-11

I believe that we should always be going forward, that we should never get to the place where we're satisfied because when we do, we let go of God. The sad thing is that many don't even realize that they are getting further and further away and threading on dangerous ground.

I always want God to be the desire of my heart. I want to know him more and more and to become more intimately acquainted with him. He is my life. The bible says in him we live and move and have our being. I can't imagine getting away from him after knowing him the way I do.

<u>Poem</u>

My Heart's Desire

Lord, you walk with me day by day.

You are my heart's desire.

You've walked with me through hard times,

You are the fourth man in the fire.

How mighty is your power, how mighty is your strength!

In the times of trouble, you are my strength within.

The tempest grows dark and the waves rise up against me,

I still have perfect peace within because my heart is stayed on thee.

You are my shelter from the storm, my safe dwelling place.

You give to me your word for strength and your amazing grace.

In times of trouble your word teaches me to praise and worship thee,

Even though at times, the way out, I cannot see.

The storms grow ominous and there's trouble all around,

I have confidence I'll always make it through.

Because:

My feet are planted on solid ground, and my faith and trust are in you.

Did Angels See?

One day as I was listening to the Christian radio station I heard a song about angels and it got me to wondering what angels really see.

How much can be seen from heaven? We know God sent angels to earth many times on special occasions and we understand that angels have been sent forth to minister for those who will inherit salvation according to Hebrews 1:14. I wonder if we being the heirs of salvation really understand that angels have been sent forth for us.

Are angels standing unemployed in heaven because their services are not being requested? How do angels receive the signal that something needs to be done on earth?

According to the bible angels hearken to the voice of his word, so it would appear that when God's word is spoken by those who are heirs of salvation, the angels go to work.

How important is it for us to speak the word instead of the problem? Many Christians dwell on their problems and want to talk about them but very seldom speak what the bible says about their problem.

> Proverbs 18:21 Death and life are in the power of the tongue,
> and those who love it will eat its fruit.

What fruit is the bible talking about? It's talking about the fruit of our lips. In our tongue lies the power of life and death. Every time we speak we are either producing the fruit of life or death. When one speaks of his or her problems all the time, that person is not getting any closer to solving his or her problem. With our words we are planting seeds that one day will produce fruit either of life or of death.

If we want a solution to our problem we must find that solution in the word of God and begin to say what God says about our situation. As we began to speak words of life seeds of life are being planted and it will produce fruit to solve our problem. If we can just understand the importance of speaking the right thing, it would save us a world of trouble. We hear so much negativism spoken today; it makes me wonder if the angels are standing by waiting for the right words to be spoken so they can go to work.

The book of Revelation speaks of how the angels fall prostrate all around the throne and worship. It makes me think that maybe they have more insight into the life and death of our Lord and Savior Jesus Christ.

Did they watch from heaven as the choice was made between Jesus and Barabbas? Did they see as Jesus was being wounded for our transgressions and bruised for our iniquities? What did they see? Did they understand the price he paid more than we do and if so is that the reason why they fall on their faces before him in worship? Are we missing something when our worship services are cold and dry and boring? Do we understand the price Jesus paid for our redemption?

God is seeking true worshippers to worship him. If he has to seek for them there must not be too many true worshippers. Worship doesn't only mean worshipping in song and lifting our hands toward heaven. Worship is a lifestyle of how we live every day. If we love the Lord our lifestyle should portray the love we have for him. A true worshipper would be a doer of the word and not just a hearer. A true worshipper worships with his spirit soul and body, loving the Lord with everything that's in him or her. He or she would put the word to work in his or her life in order to live a life that is pleasing to the Lord.

What did angels see?

Poem

Did Angels See?

Did angels see the pain and agony in the garden of Gethsemane?

Did they weep as he hung on that cross for you and me?

Did they bow their heads in reverence as darkness covered the earth?

Did they understand that all of this was leading to the new birth?

Angels rejoice when one gets born again.

Did they know that Calvary was the doorway to forgiveness of man's sin?

Were they watching from the grandstands as all of this took place?

Is that why they worship and fall prostrate on their face?

Do they understand more than we do God's amazing grace and why God sent his Son to die for the human race?

Angels came and strengthened him in the garden of Gethsemane but they couldn't prevent him from dying on Calvary because there was no other way to set the captives free.

What is a Pastor?

And he himself gave some to be apostles, some prophets, some evangelists, and some pastors and teachers, for the equipping of the saints for the work of the ministry, for the edifying of the body of Christ, till we all come to the unity of the faith and of the knowledge of the Son of God, to a perfect man, to the measure of the stature of the fullness of Christ; that we should no longer be children tossed to and fro and carried about with every wind of doctrine, by the trickery of men, in the cunning craftiness of deceitful plotting, but speaking the truth in love, may grow up in all things into Him who is the head-Christ—from whom the whole body, joined and knit together by what every joint supplies, according to the working by which every part does its share, causes growth of the body for the edifying of itself in love.
Ephesians 4:11-16

What is a pastor? That's a good question right? All of us who attend church see our pastor every time we go to church but few of us ask the question what is a pastor? What does my pastor do? What are his responsibilities? What is my pastor doing when I don't see him?

The bible tells us that God himself placed pastors in the body of Christ as part of the five-fold ministry for the job of perfecting the saints for the work of the ministry. The pastor's job is very important.

A pastor job does not consist of preparing pretty messages to please the people and then spend the rest of his free time doing nothing. A pastor has a great responsibility to God and to his flock. God has made him the overseer or the shepherd of the flock that God has entrusted him with. His job is a 24/7 job.

A pastor spends much time in prayer for his flock. When one sheep leaves the fold he goes out to find the sheep and find out why the sheep has strayed. He does his best to bring that sheep back home.

The pastor is concerned about his people. He makes sure that they get the best teaching available, that they are growing in the word and becoming productive Christians. He makes sure that each person is ministered to on his or her level of learning. He takes care of the little lambs as well as the youth and the adult. It's not an easy job being a pastor. God graces those he calls to do the job and do it with excellence. This poem was written on Pastor's appreciation Day several years ago.

Poem

What is a pastor?

A pastor is a man who's called to run a race. It takes a special person to be in the pastor's place.

Much time this man must spend in prayer, much time is spent in study.

Not to mention all that goes on behind the scenes.

Folks don't go through things alone while in the pastor's care, whatever their need the pastor is always there.

A pastor is a man that loves without restraint.

No matter how hard his race may be he's one who never faints.

Even though at times he may shed some tears, those tears will always bring wisdom through the years.

The pastor is also human and faces many trials and tests, which when allowed they make him stronger and bring out God's very best.

A better man to lead the flock, God could never find.

Twenty four seven the sheep are on his mind.

The sheep are his priority right from the start and when they are apart they are always on his heart.

Much time in the word and prayer he must spend. One of his jobs is people's hearts to mend.

The word of God says; give honor where honor is due.

Today we want to take this time to honor you. And say that we appreciate you for all the work you do.

A Tribute to Dad

For verily I say unto you, that whosoever shall say unto this mountain, be thou removed and be thou cast into the sea, and shall not doubt in his heart, but shall believe that those things which he saith shall come to pass; he shall have whatsoever he saith. Mark 11:23

Many men and women live and die and never leave a legacy, then there are great men and women who touched countless lives and even after death the legacy goes on.

Brother Kenneth E. Hagin was one of those kinds of persons that impacted my life. I was influenced by his books long before I attended Rhema. I was privileged to attend Rhema Bible Training Center in 1990 and 91 while Brother Hagin was still alive. I was privileged to receive some of my training from his classes. I also was privileged to attend several of his Holy Ghost meetings throughout the United States and to see firsthand the move of the Holy Spirit.

There are certain things he said that stayed with me. I believe his favorite scripture was Mark 11:23. He always quoted it and talked about how many times the scripture says, say and believe. The importance of what we say and what we believe was ingrained in my spirit. I heard it so many times. I understand that it's possible to doubt in your head and still believe in your heart. I also believe that there are times that we need to speak to the mountains in our life and they will be removed if we don't doubt in our heart. Then there are times that we need to pray about certain things. Things we speak to are things God has already given us authority over or he has said they belong to us.

I will always remember Brother Hagin as a man who walked in love. I learned many things about walking in love from watching and hearing him.

He always admonished us to be quick to repent and quick to forgive.

I recall the many times he said, "Don't believe anything because I said it, search the scriptures and prove it out for your own self." He taught us to study the word for ourselves in order to not be deceived by doctrines of man. Being human any one of us can miss it. Another thing I remember was what he said every time he prayed for the sick. He'd say "Jesus is the healer." He believed and practiced what the scripture says about laying hands on the sick and they shall recover. Many were healed by the laying on of hands during his years of ministry.

Many prophecies were given by him that came to pass. One thing he always said "if it bears witness with your spirit take it if not I'm human and I can miss it."

The last thing I recall that he said to us was "you can't just have the word alone; you need the Holy Spirit too. It has to be the word and the Holy Spirit working together." For many years ministers placed the emphasis on the word and many of us learned the importance of the word and putting it to work in our life, but in so doing we left the Holy Spirit out. Brother Hagin was very concerned that this generation was going to lose the move of the Spirit if we didn't have the word and the Spirit working together. In our excitement about the word we left the Holy Spirit out and instead of allowing the Spirit to work the word we tried to do it ourselves. That's why for many the word of God is not working in their life.

For there are three that bear witness in heaven: the Father, the Word, and the Holy Spirit; and these three are one. I John 5:7

Brother Hagin founded Rhema Bible Training Center in 1974. Since then Rhema has graduated over 30,000 graduates. Rhema also has several foreign Rhema Bible Training Centers in other countries.

Brother Hagin passed in September of 2003, he was 86 years old. He was a great loss to many people all over the world and to all those graduates who called him "Dad." We know that one day we will be united in heaven. The bible says to be absent from the body is to be present with the Lord. One day there will be a great reunion up in heaven.

I take great honor in having this opportunity to honor the memory of a man who helped multitudes of people. The bible says we should honor and esteem them highly. This poem was written in his memory.

I Timothy 5:17 Let the elders who rule well be counted worthy of double honor, especially those who labor in the word and doctrine.

I Thessalonians 5:12-13 And we urge you, brethren, to recognize those who labor among you, and are over you in the Lord and admonish you, and to esteem them very highly in love for their work's sake. Be at peace among yourselves.

Poem

A Tribute to Dad

Many men of God have lived upon the earth and left behind a legacy of things that they have done.

But few have left behind sons and daughters whose faith has been inspired by the race this man has run, a race of faith unfeigned and a love that never ceased.

He will always be remembered by Mark 11:23

He was a man who led the race of untold believers, some of whom he never saw their face.

One day in heaven as crowns are handed out, all of those believers will rise up with a shout, and say we're here today because of a dream you had, graduates of Rhema from every tribe and land, who honored him and loved him and even called him dad.

That dream will continue until the race is run, we will take up the torch and continue to go on, messengers of glory, messengers of light, fighting every battle and winning every fight, led by the Holy Ghost empowered by his might.

Legacy

There are many people who pass through this life and never leave a legacy. Once they are gone they are soon forgotten. It's sad that many people have no goals in life. They have no vision; they merely exist from day to day.

The bible tells us that people perish because they have no vision. We need something to propel us forward, a dream to keep us going, and a goal to keep us focused.

Every time I think of dreams I'm reminded of Joseph in the bible. Joseph had a dream, a literal dream that kept him going forward no matter what tests and trials came his way. His own brothers hated him and called him the dreamer. One day they threw him into a pit and were going to leave him there to die. But as fate would have it, as they sat down to eat they lifted up their eyes and saw a company of Ishmaelites coming down from Gilead on their way to Egypt. To make a long story short they decided to sell him as a slave.

The thing I admire about Joseph is that he never gave up because things didn't go his way. He learned how to turn bad situations around for his benefit. He learned to make the best of every situation and God used the opportunity for the making of a great leader who would one day save a nation. How do we know if God is not using the opportunity of things we go through to train us for something he has called us to?

The apostle Paul was a great leader. He said "I have learned whatever state I'm in to be content." He wasn't born with the gift of contentment. It was something he learned and practiced throughout his ministry.

I want the world to know that I am passing through and one day having passed, that I was here. I want to leave a legacy of my desire to help people find hope in seemingly hopeless situations and a world full of chaos. The world we live in today offers very little hope. People are perishing every day because they have lost their hope. They feel their life is over, that there's nothing left to live for. If one can think of one thing he or she would like to accomplish in life and go for it, and stop at nothing to see that one thing come to pass, that person would be on his or her way to succeeding at something. Once a person has succeeded at one thing it is so much easier to set goals and see greater things accomplished in one's life.

Poem

Legacy

I want to leave a legacy for the entire world to see.

I want the world to know the work that God has done in me.

I want the world to know that God so loved the world, that he gave his only begotten Son.

He did it for millions; he would have done it for one.

I don't want to go through life as though I'd never been here.

I want to make an impact with what God has given me to share.

God gave gifts to men and talents too, he has planned something that only you can do.

You'll always succeed if you follow through and your dreams you continue to pursue.

God said, I set before you, life and death, cursing and blessing, choose life that you and your descendants may live.

A life abundant and full of Joy is the life that Jesus came to give.

God knows everything about you and he knows what you are going to do.

He has prepared a path that is destined just for you.

Don't ever feel that your life isn't worth much.

You were fearfully and wonderfully made, fashioned by the master's touch.

Live to leave a legacy wherever you go, you are touching people's lives more than you will ever know.

How can I say Thanks?

I sometimes marvel at the greatness of our God and the many blessings he has bestowed upon my family. I can look back to a time when we didn't know the Lord and I can see where he has brought us from. My husband and I both grew up in poverty stricken homes. We had very little of life's pleasures. When we married we lived from pay check to pay check, we were in debt and sick most of the time. We had vehicles that left us stranded on the road many times, because we either ran out of gas or had a flat tire. We had very little to offer our children.

Since we met the Lord in 1979, he has blessed us so much that we can't help but have a heart full of gratitude for the things he has done. It didn't happen all at once. We had to learn the word and then apply it to our life. We had to form a relationship with the Lord throughout the years. The more we walked in the word the more blessed we became. Now we can truly say God has blessed us abundantly. Prosperity is not measured in how much money one has. Prosperity is measured in how much of God we have and how much of his word we are putting into practice. There are many things money can't buy. I have found that there are no greater riches than living for the Lord. We have no needs because all of our needs are met. God has always been faithful to his promises.

I am forever grateful to him for the things he has done and the things he will continue to do as I follow him. I see many Christians who are very inconsiderate of others and the things others do for them. I find it hard to understand why Christians are so ungrateful. I can understand those who haven't read the word or haven't received Jesus as their Lord and

Savior, they have a legitimate excuse. The bible teaches us to imitate the Lord. I know we are living in difficult times but that's no excuse for anyone to become ungrateful. I can't thank my God enough first of all because he so loved the world that he gave his only begotten son to die for me. He saw my condition without God and had mercy upon me.

We have so much to be thankful for. The greatest thing we can do to show our gratitude is to live a life that is pleasing to the Lord. That's all that he requires of us. How hard can it possibly be to live for the Lord? He gives us the instructions in his word. All of his plans are for our good. Following the Lord has been the greatest blessing I have ever known. It has taken me down paths I never thought I would travel. It has given me confidence I never thought I could have. It has given me peace that passes all understanding even in desperate situations.

How can I say thanks for the many things he's done for me?

God is a good God and his thoughts for you are for good and not for evil according to *Jeremiah 29:11*. *For I know the thoughts that I think toward you, saith the Lord, thoughts of peace, and not of evil, to give you an expected end.*

God's desire for us is peace. There are many people in the world who have never known the peace of God. They live in impoverished nations where chaos reigns and the people know no peace. Many young people in our world today are taken as slaves to feed the cravings of lust. Lives are being destroyed at a very young age. Many times these people think they can never recover or gain back their self-respect. My heart goes out to them. I thank God that my children and grandchildren have been shielded from such a life.

I can only give the credit to God and to my Lord Jesus Christ who prayed that we would be kept from the evil in the world. I sometimes feel like I'm on the outside looking in or that I'm in a bubble of protection and I can only lift my voice in thanksgiving unto him.

Poem

How can I say Thanks?

How can I say thanks for the many things you've done for me?

How can I say thanks for the way you set the captives free?

How can I say thanks for the death you died on Calvary?

How can I say thanks for the recovery of sight you gave to me?

When I was blind you gave me sight.

When I sat in darkness you became my light.

When I was bound you set me free.

When I was lost you found me.

Where can I find the right words to say thank you?

I can only live a life that is pleasing to you and express my gratitude in the things I do.

I can lift my hands in praise and Say thank you.

I can fall prostrate on my face and worship you.

Words cannot express my gratitude, but many things can be expressed through attitude.

May we always have an attitude of thanksgiving for the things you have done.

May we always remember that you gave your only Son.

Conclusion

Poetry can express the thoughts we can't seem to put into words. I hope that these poems have been a blessing to you and that they will be an encouragement to you when you need encouragement and comfort when you need comfort.

My heart's desire is to touch the lives of as many people as I can. I can't repay the Lord for all he's done for me but I can help someone else to get closer to him. I can help someone else understand scripture. I can give people hope, something they can hang on to.

The book of Psalms is a poetic book. In it we see the writer in times of distress. We see him reaching out to God and calling upon his name. We see him singing psalms and hymns unto God when he is joyful. There were times when Israel was at war and a psalm would be written about how powerful God is in battle. There's a psalm for every occasion. Most of the book of Psalms is praise unto God, the writer expressing the thoughts of his heart to his maker.

There are many times that I write my own greeting cards because I can't seem to find what I'm looking for to express the thoughts of my heart at the time.

Many times poetry is put into music. Music has a way of touching people's hearts. People can relate to words put to music. Music is a powerful tool in the hands of a skilled musician or singer. King David wrote most of the Psalms. He was a skilled musician. I like to believe that as David was watching his father's sheep he learned to play the harp and play skillfully for the Lord. Maybe he used his music to calm the sheep. We see in Psalm 23 that he learned a lot about God as our shepherd while observing the sheep he cared for. He came to understand God's care for us. He played the harp in such a way that God anointed him to play when evil spirits were tormenting King Saul. As soon as David would begin to play the harp the evil spirits would depart.

Worship music can lead one into the presence of God. Music like poetry expresses the heart of the composer. Worship is an integral part of every believer's relationship with the Lord.

I write poetry as I feel led of the Lord. I do it to give glory to him. I would like to think that God is pleased when we take what he has given us and use it to give glory to him. I can't take any credit for the poetry I write except to put it on paper. I see poetry as a little bit of God's creative ability placed inside of me.

Poetry is one way that I can express the feelings of my heart. I didn't learn to write poetry and I don't know much about prose. I write it as it comes to me. I enjoy poetry because it expresses the heart of the writer and I can get a better feel of what that person is trying to get across.

I see Poetry as an art, a literary art. It is a gift given by the creator of all mankind. Not all use their gifts and talents to give glory to God. I'd like to believe that if God gave the gift it should be used to glorify him.

My prayer for you the reader is that these poems will minister to your heart.

I pray that you will be able to find hope even in seemingly hopeless situations. I pray that you will see God as a big God, the Almighty, and all powerful one and that you come to know how much he loves you.